NOBODY'S ever cried for me...

Dave Roever
with Karen Crews Crump

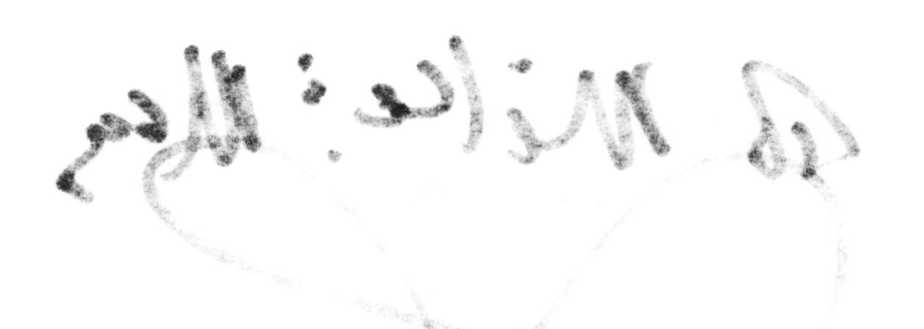

Roever Communications, a division of
Roever Evangelistic Association
P.O. Box 136130 • Fort Worth, TX 76136
(817) 238-2005

TABLE OF CONTENTS

Preface

Finally, I begin.

This is the fulfillment of a promise I made myself many years ago. I promised someday to write a book about the experiences I have had as I crisscrossed this nation bringing hope to a generation of kids in public schools.

This is not going to be a lovely story. The truth is, it will probably be an ugly story. A story of suffering, grief, and pain. The final conclusion? *It did not have to be!*

In all honesty this book does not have to be. I could suppress what I know, and how I know it, the same way kids have been doing for years. But I have used that mechanism far too long, postponing what I knew must eventually be done.

Maybe the suppression, both mine and the kids', springs from the same source. No one wants to face the reality that we have a problem in this country.

Yes, in this nation.

A nation whose money says, *In God We Trust;* whose pledge says, *One nation under God;* whose pride covers its losses in war with movies that change the outcome. There is something terribly wrong, however, when we realize in the end, we won the movie but lost the war.

A promise I will make to you now is, regardless of the outcome, regardless of the status of the all-American family's image, I will tell the truth.

His Father's Eyes

The engines purred in synchronized harmony as we cruised down the Vam Co Tay River at forty knots. July in South Vietnam is miserably hot, but this particular day the humidity must have been 99 percent. The oppressive air made me almost wish for gills to help extract oxygen from it.

Events of the night before weighed heavily on my mind. During a terrible fire fight a piece of shrapnel had cut open my cheek, and the ever-present, dull, throbbing ache in my mouth reminded me of yet another near brush with death.

Our crew of four had been patrolling the narrow river in our little fiberglass boat when the enemy opened fire. Thirteen anti-tank, B-40-type rockets were launched at us from a bunker concealed in high brush just a few yards away.

A projectile from a small-caliber rifle hit the tip of my M-60 machine gun and blew off the flash suppressor causing the damage to my cheek.

With a few stitches at an Army field hospital and a citation for a purple heart, I was sent back on patrol.

Our mission this day was to confirm intelligence reports that the enemy had pulled out of the bunker. The assignment wasn't unusual. We'd done this same thing many times, but I never got used to it. It always bothered me. Too many booby traps.

We beached the small boat on the bank of the river with the bow toward the bunker. It all seemed too easy. Nothing moved except the tall grass swaying gently in the sultry breeze.

All my life I've known to trust my instincts, and that day I had a powerful awareness of the presence of the enemy. I started to say something, but I didn't think the rest of the crew would believe me, so I said nothing.

Instead, I selected a phosphorus hand grenade which would ignite on impact, creating a white-hot flash fire to instantly denude the land and give us a clear view of the bunker. I threw the first grenade, but saw I needed another to finish the job.

I would never finish the job.

The door to death is always open. Its threshold is only one step away at any moment... one heartbeat... one bullet from a sniper's rifle. The grenade exploded in my hand.

When I was a kid, I was often told I looked like my dad. That had always been my greatest source of pride, my heritage from my dad, a proof of ownership or legitimacy. It was the evidence of roots.

This physical documentation was, however, shared with my brother, Al. Al was such an avowed individualist, though, he would never admit to even the slightest resemblance, regardless of glaring evidence.

It was the jaw. That telltale, ninety-degree jut of bone, just like Dad's. The teeth mark us, too — a gap between the two front teeth, seemingly big enough to drive a truck through — just like Dad's.

And just like Dad, both of us have stubborn, never-admit-you're-wrong, unconquerable spirits that make us drive on down the road, claiming, "Oh, I just wanted to see the neighborhood," when the wife points out we just missed our street.

The hairline, the eyes, the nose, the ears, the voice, all are evidence of belonging to someone you love. Yet, with all the sameness, there is still the unmistakable you. The one, the only you. The one people will say your kids look just like. And it's always the face people are referring to. They never look at your feet and declare your likeness to the family photo. It's the face.

But what happens when the face is blown away with a grenade? When it's mutilated beyond recognition, and you look in a mirror and can't recognize yourself? Where's the likeness to Dad then? Where's the feeling of security you always had, knowing you looked just like Papa? Where's your self-confidence?

Gone.

Heads turn, and you hear people whisper so loudly you get the impression they think you're deaf as well as scarred. Each glance, every word cutting deeper into the soul, driving you into the ground, and you claw at the hole, trying to pull it in behind you.

Scars that you feel will never go away begin to be the determining factor in your decision-making process.

To avoid embarrassment, you stay home instead of enjoying the social interaction found in going to church, going to fun places, or going shopping. You start to hate yourself, feeling ugly and rejected.

Thoughts of suicide make you afraid of being alone, but alone is about all you are these days.

Something is happening. Something awful, something terribly wrong is happening. Those scars are moving, being transferred from the body to the soul to be locked away to bleed in solitude. They bleed in the night when darkness allows you the only look at them. Sometimes they shock you when they unexpectedly appear at the slightest provocation.

You lie. It's the only way to cover the pain and excuse the tears that threaten to unmask you. Say it's the carpet, the paint, the cat that makes your eyes water, anything. But don't let anyone know how much it hurts.

It's been twenty-some years now, and I've learned things that only time and experience can teach. I can't help but laugh when I read psychology books filled with mechanical terms which are applied to the inner workings of the soul. Formulas demand certain responses to given circumstances, and the expected never fails; e.g., "When great physical trauma is sustained, one is psychologically raped, and therefore, will be functionally handicapped for life."

How can a man go through all this suffering of body and soul and not vomit from soul-bitterness, hatred, vengeance, violence, and who knows what else? What stops him from suicide? From beating his wife? Molesting his kids? Or abusing drugs? Why doesn't he blame God?

Well, my face is half gone. I wear a plastic ear and synthetic hairpiece. My left thumb came out of my right hip. My right thumb from my left hip. My upper-right eyelid came from my lower-right side. My lower lid from my upper-left shoulder. My face came off my legs — it was the doctors' second choice — the first choice I declined because you wouldn't know if I were coming or going. I'm scattered all over myself!

But my soul is not scarred. My spirit is not patched together. I can laugh. I can enjoy life. And I can share my life and laughter with hurting people — unforgettable people — as you will soon see.

Captain Crunch

I hate being told, "No."

All my life it's bothered me. When people have said, "You can't," I've set out to prove that I can.

Week after week I lay in my hospital bed feeling helpless and almost hopeless. All I needed to make my day was some over-zealous staff psychologist who thought she knew it all to step up to my bed and say to her assistant, "This one is psychologically raped. He'll never be anything."

The woman who made the pronouncement was an Army captain. You know...two bars on her hat and everything. She was also our physical therapist. She crunched on our brains, and she crunched on our fingers. We called her *Captain Crunch*.

Charred black from my waist up, skinless arms suspended on pads at the elbows, face half-gone and the half that was left swollen to my shoulder, already depressed from the pain, and what did she say?

"He'll never be anything."

Well, she shouldn't hadn't ort'a done that!

I went crazy! Her words ignited my powder keg. How dare she say that in my presence! Who does she think she is?

"I will be something!" I thought, "I will be something!" Suddenly I realized I wasn't just thinking those words; I was screaming them!

Outraged by her audacity, I leaped out of my bed. When I did, the surface of my raw back stuck to the sheet. It felt like I was being skinned alive which infuriated me that much more.

I was nose to nose with her, my undamaged nostril flaring and my entire body trembling with rage. I shook my fist at her and screamed in her face, "I will be something! I will be something!"

Then stitches started popping. On my right hand three fingers and my thumb broke loose and dangled by tendons. The stitches in an artery deep in my hand broke at the same time, and blood pumped out of it in spurts, spraying Captain Crunch's face and blouse.

"Don't tell me I won't be anything!" I bellowed. "I will be something!"

At that instant I noticed the strange pattern the spurts of blood had created on her blouse. A large "Z" stretched across her chest. Zorro strikes again!

Her mouth fell open as she stood momentarily in a state of shock, but as reality set in, she started shrieking. Her notes went straight up into the air a few micro-seconds ahead of her body. Then she hit the floor in a dead run for the border, screaming all the way.

"Wow," I thought, "I told her!"

Then I noticed it. I was naked — buck naked!

I didn't have any clothes on. I didn't know that! Why didn't they put clothes on me? Still bleeding profusely, I jumped back into bed. Frantically fumbling with the sheets, I finally managed to pull them over me enough, so I didn't feel exposed to the world.

Hearing all the commotion, nurses came running. They put pressure on the artery to stop the bloodletting and called the doctor to tend to my fingers.

The nurses were a bit shocked to see me grinning. They asked why, but I knew they wouldn't believe me if I told them.

Why wouldn't they believe me?

From the time of my injury until Captain Crunch declared I'd never be anything, I'd never gotten out of bed by myself. Until that moment, I'd never stood on my own two feet without somebody holding me up.

And... I was something. Even if it was naked!

Boy, did I show her!

Assume the Position

Someone once said, "A man with an experience is never at the mercy of a man with an argument." For many years I've believed that philosophy, and in pursuing it, I've often found myself on the losing end of an experience.

This is another of those experiences which would so drastically change my life. At the time, though, I never dreamed it was having such an effect.

Life doesn't always present a *Foreword* or a neatly prepared outline to help predict the next event. Just when you think it's okay to go outside in the dark... Well, this story takes place in the dark.

It was a Sunday night in the inner city of Minneapolis. The church was a renovated theater, and it was packed full with standing room only. The congregation was one of those exciting, clap-your-hands, sing-all-night kind, and they received me like a much-loved family member.

I shared with them the story of my injury and recovery, explaining how God kept me through the ordeal although I'd escaped with little more than my humor intact.

The people were right with me. They laughed, they cried, and the program ended with a bang. Afterward, they bought every book and tape I had to sell — hundreds of dollars worth.

I so enjoyed the church... after all, they bought all my stuff. That seemed a good sign of God's approval of *my ministry*.

I'm not sure I knew what a ministry was at that time. The only way I knew to judge my success was by holding my ministry up against that of others. I could always find someone who would make me look good in comparison.

After getting my things together, I waited in the foyer for the pastor to take me to a hotel. It grew late. Nearly all the people had gone by the time he finally came. He hurried over to me and said he had a quick board meeting to conduct, but assured me it wouldn't take long.

Quick board meeting? No way. I knew I was in for a long wait, so to pass the time I strolled outside to get some fresh air. In any inner city that's like breathing up the tail pipe of a bus.

I stepped out the door and passed through the twilight zone into another dimension of time and space. The air was biting — colder than normal for the season — but that wasn't the problem. As night settled over the city and happy church members were inside singing praises to God, the scene outside the church door had changed dramatically.

I was totally unprepared for what met my eyes.

There were probably a hundred to a hundred-fifty men lining the gutter and sidewalk, sitting there with bottles in hand, staring blankly into the darkness.

I'd never been to skid row. I'd never been to an inner city before that night. This was a strange new world to me.

Dumbfounded, I must have stood there staring at the spectacle for several minutes before I realized the immensity of the social and spiritual problem staring back at me. Staggered by the implications, I sagged against the church wall.

"Jesus," I thought, "If you were here tonight, which side of this concrete wall would you be standing on?"

I knew the answer before I asked. *He came not for the well, but rather, for the sick.*

Then what was I doing in there preaching to the ones who wore nice clothes; who drove nice cars to nice homes to sleep in nice beds; who would awaken to eat good food and go to work at good jobs and receive good paychecks to support their good lives?

None of these things are evil. I was simply confronted for the first time in my life with the futility of what I was doing and the purpose for which I was doing it.

Rather than debate the issue before me, I decided to experience it. I rushed back into the church lobby, took off my coat and tie, pulled out my shirt tail, took off my cuff-links, rolled up my sleeves, mussed my hair piece, and headed for the gutter.

When I was fifteen-years-old, two friends of mine came to tell me they'd found someone to buy their beer for them. "Hey, Dave, we've got some booze and women!" they boasted.

I looked them straight in the eye and said, "Yeah, and you don't know what to do with either one of them."

What's a fifteen-year-old boy going to do with a woman? He thinks he knows, but he's never pulled the tail of a sleeping mountain lion either.

What was I doing in a gutter with hardened alcoholics and drug users? I thought I knew. I thought I could get a course in human understanding in three easy lessons.

I pulled my feet under me as I sat down next to a drunk. He seemed a nice enough guy — even offered me a swig on his bottle. I figured I'd come this far, I might as well take the bottle.

I couldn't bring myself to take a drink, though, so I returned it to him. He thanked me, took a long drink, and handed it back. I thanked him and returned it to him. He took another long drink and handed it back. I thanked him and returned it. He took another long drink, and it dawned on me, "The guy is going to pass out if I don't quit taking his bottle!"

As my new buddy and I were passing his bottle back and forth, I became aware of someone standing right in front of me. I looked up into the faces of a steely-blue-eyed, toothless man and his woman companion.

They interrupted our moment of sharing by asking my buddy where the soup line was. When he told them, they said they'd just come from there, and the place was closed.

Without hesitation my buddy reached into his shirt and retrieved a sandwich. Pimento cheese. I could smell it. They exude a distinct odor when going bad.

The man in front of me threw up his hands and said, "Naw, man, we can't take that! You stood in line all day to get it."

Suddenly the woman reached out and snatched the sandwich. Her words cut through me. "I'm not proud; I'm hungry."

I couldn't believe what was happening. This was ripping apart my social conscience. I didn't want to be there any more. I wanted to erase everything I was seeing and hearing. I looked around; there was no way out. I was hemmed in.

But I had to leave. There was enough money in my pocket from sales that night to feed the entire lot of them for a week. I couldn't afford to get too involved; it might cost me something.

Too late.

The sound of screeching tires and yelling voices abruptly brought an end to my thoughts. Blue lights flashed, and uniformed officers leaped from their cars shouting, "Assume the position!"

What position? Do I stand? Kneel? Sit? Lie down? What do they want? It only took a minute to learn.

Everyone else knew what to do. They faced the church building and leaned forward. Placing their hands on the wall and setting their feet spread-eagle, they yielded to the officers who frisked them.

An officer looked at me and barked, "Who do you think you are? Assume the position!"

Hot flashes swept over me. I heard the sound of my own voice pleading, "I'm not one of them! You can't do this to me! I don't belong here! I'm a preacher!"

"Assume the position!"

"I don't think you heard me," I said. "I'm not one of them."

"You didn't hear *me*!" the officer shot back. "I told you to assume the position. If you don't, I'm taking you downtown!"

I wasn't sure what "downtown" meant. I thought I was downtown, but if it were worse than this, I didn't want to go there. I assumed the position.

I didn't think I would like the position, and I was right. Being frisked is an invasion of privacy, a demeaning act.

I endured it, all the time hearing my mind playing back my wimpy denials... *"I'm not one of them. You can't do this to me. I don't belong here. I'm a preacher..."*

The police collected all the bottles of liquor and poured the contents into the storm drain, as crying broken men looked on in horror.

When they finished, the police left, and so did the bums. All except one, that is. The one who really deserved to be there. The one who denied all the rest.

Then I remembered the man and woman who had asked for the soup line. Where were they during the frisking?

I searched for them in the darkness. And there they were, in the alley behind the church... sharing bites of the pimento cheese sandwich.

I couldn't take it any more, nor could I stop myself from the inevitable. I reached into my pocket and pulled out a roll of money big enough to choke a horse. I held it out to the man whose piercing eyes never blinked as he reached out and took it. Were these his father's eyes?

I told him to buy the woman the best meal she'd ever eaten and to buy her some clothes; the money was all his. He closed his hands around the money without ever averting his penetrating gaze. I felt the hair on my neck standing up.

Sometimes I hesitate to tell what happened next. I'm afraid you'll think I'm a nut. But, after what I did with that roll of money, you probably already think I am one.

I took two, maybe four steps and looked back over my shoulder. I felt my heart skip a beat. They were gone. Not a trace of them or the money.

I returned to the church lobby, tucked in my shirt, put on my tie and coat, combed my hair, and right on cue, the pastor stepped out.

"Let's go," he said. "I told you it wouldn't take long." Then he called for his car to come.

When it arrived, I was speechless. There before me, where moments earlier a pack of filthy, hungry beggars had sat, was a long black limousine.

My first thought was, "No way am I getting into that car! This has been a strange enough night. How much more can I stand?"

They took me to the Hilton to a room so big it seemed to take up half the top floor. The bed was turned down, and a wine bottle sat beside a crystal glass on the table. Near it lay a note which read, "If you need anything, call Sherrie."

All I could think about were those people on the street. Who could they call?

I refused to sleep in the bed. My conscience wouldn't let me. I lay on the floor and cried out to God. I asked Him to give me a ministry that would make a difference. Not a ministry to please Christians, but one that would turn the lives of the hopeless around before they landed on skid row!

My mind began to race. I saw a huge garbage can filled with ministries that others had thrown away — trashed because they were not spectacular or because they weren't glorious causes. Ministries with no money in them — garbage can ministries, all of them.

I closed my eyes and in my mind, I saw myself reach into the can and grab the first one I touched. I pulled out the worst of all. Public schools. The one place where preachers are hated the most. The least likely place to ever hope for acceptance. And as for money and fame? Not on your life.

I made a choice that night. If public schools were where God wanted me, then public schools were where I would be found.

What if.....

On the day Pilate tried Christ,
When they whipped Him with the cat-o'-nine-tails,
When they placed a crown of thorns on His head,

What if.....

When they led Him down the Via Dolorosa
With a cross on His back,
When they laid Him down on the cross,
Raised the hammer high,
Pressed the nails in place,

What if.....

He had said, "Hold everything!
You can't do this to me. I don't belong here.

I'm not one of them.
I'm the preacher........"

Thank God. He spread His arms, and He assumed the position!

And just for the record, I won't be surprised at all if, after spending some wonderful moments with Christ in heaven, I turn to face a steely-blue-eyed, toothless angel who is holding a fistful of dollars and a bunch of checks drawn on the banks of Minneapolis.

Wrong Tube

As I travel around the country speaking in schools, a question kids commonly ask is, "Was the day on the river in Vietnam the worst day of your life?"

I always struggle with that question. Was it worse than the day I got my draft notice and began all this? Was it worse than the first day of boot camp without which none of the traumatic events in my life could have occurred? Maybe the worst day of my life is yet to be lived, and I don't know it.

Ugh! I don't even want to think about that possibility.

There are days in my memory which can compete quite well in the race for *Worst Day*, but to pick one day... well, I guess I have to go to Japan for that.

First, let me go back to the bank of the river in Vietnam.

Any time a hand grenade blows off 40 percent of your skin and 60 pounds of flesh, that could be called a bad day. I was left blind in my right eye. My right ear was burned off as was my right eyelid. My fingers dangled by tendons and blood was running everywhere.

Yep, no question about it, that was a bad day.

But not bad enough to want to kill myself. I wanted to live, not die. I tried to save my life, not take it. I wasn't looking for a way out, but rather, a way to survive.

That would change.

Only one time as a boy did the thought of suicide enter my mind. When I was born, my mother's health was so seriously damaged she never fully recovered.

I lived the first 38 years of my life never knowing if she would make it to the next day. I'd come home from school thinking I'd find her dead on the floor or dead in her bed. On several occasions she looked too-far-gone for me to have any hope for her survival. Every time, though, she would somehow pull out of it.

At the age of nine I passed the open door of my parents' bedroom and inadvertently overheard them talking about mom's health. Dad was recalling the order of events of her sickness.

"Lois, Darling, your health used to be good, but it's been going downhill ever since Davey-boy was born."

All I heard was what any boy would hear in his own immature way. "It's my fault Mom is sick all the time! I'm to blame. If I'd never been born, Mom would be fine today. Maybe I should kill myself, then she'll get better."

My father never knew I heard him that day, and I'm glad. He certainly didn't mean those words to say what my young mind heard.

Years later I would have another serious confrontation with suicide in what may very well be the worst day of my life.

The Army hospital in Japan was the stop-over point for military personnel severely wounded in Vietnam. There they were stabilized before being shipped to the U.S. Many never stabilized. They died in Japan, away from the men with whom they served and away from the families they wanted so desperately to see. Halfway between heaven and hell...more hell than heaven.

It was in Japan I asked for a mirror. I wanted to get a look at the damage the Vietcong had done to my face. I don't know who was more stupid: me for asking for the mirror, or them for bringing it to me.

More than two decades later, the memory of that grotesque image staring back at me from the mirror still haunts me. I couldn't believe what I saw. It was beyond Hollywood's best efforts to make a monster. I couldn't recognize anything of myself...it wasn't me! Terror gripped me. I stared at the swollen monstrosity. The lips and flesh were stripped away, leaving a gaping, half-learing contortion.

Search as I might, I couldn't find an eyeball among the globs of charred-black flesh, cracked and oozing, where the right side of my face had once been. The white traces of zinc-oxide ointment only served to make the image more gruesome. I felt my head swimming as sickening reality came crashing in... ***it was me.***

But the worst was yet to come.

I'm the guy who never tried things which messed with my brain — drugs, alchohol, things like that. I couldn't stand the thought of losing something which couldn't be replaced. I never took a drug in my life. I could probably have taken a half-dose of Saint Joseph's aspirin for children and hallucinated for a week.

Not knowing my body's intolerance of drugs, the medics in Japan apparently overdosed me with morphine, the pain-killing drug most commonly used in hospitals for the wounded. As the drug clouded my thinking, I began to sink into a deep, dark depression. A feeling of hopelessness settled over me, out of which I felt there would be no escape.

A hideous wisp-of-a-creature stood at my bedside and hissed, "Kill yourself, you half-headed freak, and get out of your wife's misery!"

Would this be the worst day of my life?

My gaze fixed on some undetermined spot on the wall as I reached over to the only tube within my grasp. I slowly and deliberately wound it around my middle finger, then gave it a yank. One swift move, and I watched the life-giving fluids run out onto the floor. I laid my head back and waited to die.

In my ignorance, I pulled out the wrong tube.

Boy, am I glad! The years since then have been fun-filled, rich, rewarding, life-at-its-fullest, inexplicable years — years I wouldn't trade for any other face or body.

What Satan intended for evil, God has used for good. Year after year, as I share my story in high schools, kids are confronted with their own thoughts of suicide. Rarely does a day in a school pass without someone coming to me and saying, "Mr. Roever, I wanted to kill myself, too. But you made it with all your problems. So, I believe I can make it, too."

Batman In Drag

The snow crackled under the tires as we backed out of the parking space at the hotel. It was 7 a.m. and school busses were rolling all over Denver. By the time the busses unloaded at the various schools, I would be at school, too.

I would speak for four or five high school assemblies, to some seven thousand or more students by the time the last bell rang. Back then, that was just another typical school day for me.

The driver of the car, a youth pastor from a local church, looked as though he'd just crawled out of bed. I always get a kick out of taking youth pastors with me to schools. They start out at a hundred-miles-an-hour for the first two days. Then a noticeable change takes place. They slow to a mere fifty-miles-per-hour. By the end of the fourth day, I start hearing things like, "How do you do it? Three days, and I'm shot!"

We arrived at the first school about fifteen minutes early to set up the sound system. As we finished, students began pouring into the auditorium. Punk music was at its peak across America in those days, and the audience that morning had its fair share of self-styled emulators of punk.

The principal introduced me.

I spoke of my injuries in Vietnam and talked about scars. As I spoke of the suffering, I could tell by the audience's response I was touching a nerve.

The students sat on the edges of their seats with tears in their eyes as I told about the mental and physical agony I endured lying in a hospital in Japan. They became almost mesmerized as I talked about wanting to take my life when I saw my face in a mirror for the first time...

"When I saw what was left of my face, I reached up, grabbed the closest tube, and yanked it out. I wanted to die. I wanted to end it all."

They sat stunned when I calmly told how I laid my head back on the bed and waited to die.

To punkers, there is nothing worse than allowing some over-the-hill, overweight, overbearing veteran to get to you. It was too late. They were in the palm of my hand, and I knew it. Worse still, they knew that I knew it!

As they were sitting there helplessly engrossed, waiting to hear of a near brush with death in a suicide attempt, I said, "I laid my head back on my pillow, and I waited to die... But I got hungry. I'd pulled the wrong tube — I'd pulled out lunch!"

It was like letting go of the rope in a tug-o-war. They almost fell out of their chairs as pent-up emotion erupted in laughter.

How can this be? Crying one minute and laughing the next?

Then I spoke of love. Of how my teenaged wife stood at my bed and read the charts to be sure I was her man. Of how she took a long look into my one uninjured eye, then bent down and kissed my hideous face and said, "I just want you to know, I really love you. Welcome home, Davey!"

I closed the assembly and was glad to be finished. It was so hot on stage I felt nauseated. I needed air. But I stayed long enough to visit with the kids and hug the ones who waited in line, then the students had to go to class.

Not all could go immediately. Some had to take a cigarette break.

I wanted a fresh-air break, so I stepped out the back-stage door into a brilliant Denver day. The sun reflecting off the snow was so bright, it took several seconds for my eyes to adjust. When things came into focus, I saw I had a problem.

There in front of me, blocking my way, were fifteen punkers — all guys, I think. They had their heads shaved on both sides leaving a crop of yellow, green, purple, and pink hair right over the middle of their heads. They looked like a bunch of NBC peacocks gone to roost.

All of them were dressed in black with painted faces, eye shadow, mascara, lipstick, tattoos, and earrings that didn't match.

"Oh, no!" I thought, "It's Batman in drag!"

Then from somewhere in the back of my mind, a sound I was hearing, registered. Ever-so-slowly, the closing mechanism on the door behind me was about to shut off my only means of escape. I grabbed for the door. Too late. There was an unmistakable click, and I was locked out.

The tall one's eyes narrowed to slits as he looked at me. He seemed unsure of his next move.

Without warning he opened his arms wide, his long overcoat hanging to his high-top booties. I stiffened, not knowing what to expect.

"Can I hug you?" he asked.

My first reaction went back to military days and military words. I thought, "Negatory!"

Then I saw it. Little silvery pearls began to appear on the lower lid of each eye. Tears swelled and crashed over the dam of all his resistance. They ran down his powdered face and splashed in brown splotches on his black lapel.

Time stood still as I looked into his eyes. Did he look like his dad? It would be hard to tell now, I thought. You know, the eyes, the ears, those indisputable markings of the family tree. If there were a heritage there, would he want it? Would he claim it?

A voice inside me began to speak the words of an old gospel song, "For those tears I died." The words drowned out my prejudices.

I opened my arms and stood there, emotions threatening to shatter my reserve.

Like a long-lost friend, he fell into my arms. A wash of tears soaked my sleeve as he sobbed. Then he spoke softly, "Not very long ago, my sister committed suicide on this very spot where we're standing."

He went on, "You're the only person who has ever offered a word of hope to us students. Thank you for coming here today."

One lesson I've learned about punkers is, when you hug one, they all pile on. Fourteen human beings landed on top of us all at once. I went to my knees holding on to *Batman*, listening to boys weeping.

Tears flowed, mascara ran... I felt like Boy George at a family reunion!

"Guys," I said, "will you follow me in a prayer?"

"Mister, we'll follow you anywhere!"

And they did. They followed me all the way to Calvary!

Today, Batman has finished four years of Bible college and is serving Christ in full-time ministry.

Welcome Home, Davey

Ward 14-A, the intensive-care unit of the intensive-care ward at Brooke Army Medical Center in San Antonio, Texas, handles the worst cases in the field of burn medicine. I spent more than a year of my life there.

I wasn't alone in this living hell. The tortures of Dante's Inferno could hardly compare with life on 14-A. Day after day, week after week, month after month, the dozen-or-so semblances of humanity writhed in agony. Loathsome suffering eroded the spirit. The stench, like the screams, ate at the soul.

The stories of the men on the ward were as unique as the men themselves. Some were blown apart by land mines, some by hand grenades just as I was, some burned in helicopter crashes, and others burned in freak accidents — things like motorcycle wrecks and children playing with matches. All occurrences left the same evidence of trauma... scars.

For me, the scars covered the entire right side of my face where the flesh had been blown off; my back where white-hot phosphorous poured down it; my chest which had been blown open exposing my insides, and, of course, my mutilated arms and hands.

As I lay in unbelievable pain, my greatest worry was not about what part of me worked or what part didn't. It was about Brenda. I was afraid she wouldn't want me anymore.

The man in the bed next to mine was burned one-hundred-percent, third-degree. He had no skin left. There was no way he could live.

A human being cannot sustain burns of that magnitude and survive. His wife had to have known that. But she walked into the room, took off her wedding ring, dropped it between his charred feet, and said, "I couldn't walk down the street with you," then turned and walked out.

He was the first of twelve to die. In fact, they all died. Of the thirteen men who were shipped home from Vietnam together, I was the only one who survived.

When I saw the woman wheel around and leave without a backward glance, I thought, "Dear God, what will Brenda do? Will she reject the monster in front of her just like that man's wife did? Will she take off her wedding ring and drop it between my feet?"

The next person to enter the room was a teenager. Her husband in no way resembled the man she'd said good-bye to at the airport several months earlier.

She bent down and kissed what was left of my face and said, "I just want you to know, I really love you. Welcome home, Davey."

Instantaneously a miracle took place. For the first time, I didn't feel ugly. Her love made me feel handsome. Well, at least she made me feel un-ugly. Her love made my scars go away!

It's true. Scars practically cover my entire body, but it's not what you or anyone else sees. I'm the one who counts at this point, and I feel handsome. I will, therefore, behave the way I feel.

If the love of Brenda can make my scars go away, how much more can love for each other, not to mention the love of God, heal the scars of this generation?

Sarah

The names of the victims in the stories in this book have been changed to protect the guilty. They are guilty, and some are in the process of being prosecuted for criminal behavior. For that reason the names of their cities have also been changed. However, the stories are the truth, so help me God.

Time after time, it's the same old story, and you'd think one would get tired of hearing it. Tired is not the word. Angry is more accurate. Enraged is also a fair description. How long can it go on?

I'm talking about sexual abuse and forced incest upon the children of America.

Some time ago, I visited a community not too different from many others in this country. It's a mountain community which shares some unique traits with other mountainous areas. I've learned many things in my travels. Some are obvious, and some are just weird.

More than any other areas, the mountainous regions of this nation have higher numbers of students who tell me about incest. Why?

Could it be because mountainous regions attract huge numbers of followers of New-Age religions? Or because there are higher concentrations of Satanists in these areas? In both cults, moral and spiritual values based on Judeo/Christian principals are ignored. The product is obvious.

In public schools, the smelting pot of Americana, every consequence of behavior in parents is reflected in their children. Philosophies which tend to justify deviant or anti-social behavior are always incrementally acted out by the next generation.

Each new generation is constantly seeking to find the limits and parameters of behavior. They want to know how far they can go and still find that the benefits exceed the punishment for a certain action taken.

In simple terms, the world is not getting better and better. Anyone, except for the willingly stupid, will admit the world is obviously falling apart. The cost in terms of human suffering is staggering. And, unfortunately, that cost is being leveled against those least prepared to pay the price: teenagers.

Sarah is a case in point.

After delivering a public-school assembly address entitled *Scars*, I met her. During my speech I'd referred to scars of two different kinds: scars on the inside — emotional scars, and scars on the outside — physical scars from bodily injury.

Sarah wanted to talk, so she waited until everyone else had finished their conversations with me and left. Only my party and the principal of the school remained in the auditorium. Approaching like an abused puppy, Sarah shuffled up, head down and hands tightly clasped in front of her. With blonde hair and green eyes that should have been dancing with life, she was really quite attractive.

We shared light conversation for a few minutes, but I could tell she wanted to say more. Our schedule of other school assemblies that morning pressed us to go, so I invited her to the evening rally. I hated to leave her because I knew she wanted to talk. I never guessed why.

In schools, I am allowed to talk to the kids on mental and emotional levels only. Christian kids pick up on the spiritual aspect of my life right away, simply by sensing the Spirit of God within me. The other kids just know there is something different about me.

If I'm allowed the opportunity at the end of an assembly, I announce the night rally and invite the kids to come hear the rest of my story. I'm up-front with them and tell them it will be a religious function, and I will talk about my relationship with God and Jesus Christ.

The night rallies are wonderful because I don't have to rush off to other functions. I have time to listen to the students who want to talk, and I can pray with the ones who want prayer.

After the meetings I've made it a policy to stay on the stage, or near the stage area, in order to be accessible. There is another reason I stay up front: when kids hug me, and I hug them, there is never an occasion for accusations or misunderstandings because it takes place in full view of hundreds of people.

For whatever reason, this particular night I did something I never do. I slipped away from the crowd and moved to the back of the auditorium, then out into the hallway.

There she was, standing alone in a crowd of a thousand people, staring at her feet. I knew she wasn't expecting me to find her because I never do what I was doing. I was not supposed to be back there.

I stepped over to her and slipped my hand into hers. She looked up.

"Are you all right?" I asked. I could see she'd been crying, and I knew why. She'd just returned from the counseling room where the young people assisting me had prayed with her.

"Yes", she said, "I'm fine."

"Wanna talk?"

There was an awkward silence, then she reached into her purse and handed me a folded, crumpled piece of paper with a poem written on it. A poem revealing the heinous crimes committed against her. I still have that poem.

Her story is painful beyond measure.

As we talked, she bared her soul. "More than anything else in life, I want to kill my dad."

I stood shocked but kept my composure, not wanting to interrupt her.

She stumbled on, "Since I was two-years-old, he's sexually abused me...it's always happened to me...all my life. I can't remember what happened when I was two, but my mom told me he did."

"Dear God," I thought, "her mother knew and did nothing about it!"

Pandora's box could not compete with what followed. Her brothers were involved. Her father's brother and his two boys were involved, so was a man whose name she never learned. Some encounters were occasional, some only once, some with evil regularity.

"Seven men, seven deaths," was the way Sarah described the ordeals she endured at the hands of these men.

Where could she go? Who could she tell? Who would not hold it against her if they knew? Or, worse yet, what would happen if the one she confided in divulged these crimes to officials, and they confronted her father, and he took it out on her?

Then there's the biggest problem of all, self acceptance. How does a girl forget the past and relate to a husband or even to her own children one day? Does she just turn off the memories when moments of intimacy should be without intrusions from the past?

It doesn't work that way. The seething hatred, the memories, the fear, the self rejection, the rejection by others, the strong urge to self destruct, all add up to scars. Ugly, miserable, scars.

Scars don't just disappear on their own. It's not enough to bid a person, "God speed, be warmed and filled." (James 2:16) Somewhere, you have to stop and get involved. You gotta cry with them, hold them, stop giving advice and listen. Then you go for help and pay the bill.

Sarah could never afford the cost of counseling, so I arranged for the bills to be paid by a third party. Sarah doesn't know who is paying the bill. It doesn't matter. What matters is, she is being healed of those terrible and disfiguring scars on her soul. The chain is being broken in her generation, so she will not pass on the abuse to her children.

Like a dear friend of mine whose mother was a prostitute says, "Because your mother is, doesn't mean you are. And because your father did, doesn't mean you will."

Sarah is in good hands now, and I feel I have helped the next generation as well.

Welcome home, Sarah!

Nobody's Ever Cried for Me...

As I spoke for an outstanding high school assembly in Oregon, the students were giving me a hundred-ten-percent attention. They were so alive it seemed I was only getting started when I realized my allotted time was half-gone.

I had become so emotionally involved with the students that I broke and wept before them.

I spoke of love and healing for the human spirit. I told the kids that divine love restores broken human spirits — and that human love, in its purest form, can help restore broken spirits.

At the conclusion of the assembly a counselor and one of the high school girls came and asked if I could meet with them privately. Together, we walked to the counselor's office, and when we'd stepped inside, the counselor closed the door. It was then I turned and looked into the eyes of a bruised, hurting soul.

During the assembly all the walls in her young heart had come down. Now sitting in the counselor's office, she began to talk to me about her father. I could sense hatred for the man rising in her as she spoke. Tears streamed down her cheeks.

She poured out the long-pent-up story of the abuse she had endured — sexual abuse, repulsive abuse. Abuse at the hands of the man who should have been caring for her and nurturing her to maturity and adulthood.

The counselor buried his face in his hands. Tears dripped through his fingers. His shoulders heaved.

As the girl spoke, I quietly wept with her and took mental notes so I could respond. I listed in my mind all the things I wanted to say to her.

When she finished, and I was finally ready to speak, I removed my glasses to dry my eyes. Before I could, her trembling hand reached to my face and wiped my tears away.

"Nobody's ever cried for me before," she whispered. "Nobody's ever said they loved me before... You know.... what you said to us today in the assembly will live in my heart forever."

Raw emotion hung in the air as she searched for words to express herself. "I can feel your scars with my hands, and I know you suffer lots of pain... but you're making it. And if you can make it," she paused, "I know I can make it, too."

The glances I was getting from the counselor left me with the impression that this was the first time the girl had made any positive move toward opening up to anyone.

Then I spoke to the girl about Christ. You see, I was in the counselor's office by invitation. There were no limitations put on what I could say to her.

"I have also touched the scars and felt the pain of Someone I love," I said. "His name is Jesus. He understands all your anguish, but He can go beyond understanding.

"Believe me, I understand. And your counselor understands, but we can't heal you. Only Jesus Christ can do that."

The girl made no outward response to Jesus. She made no verbal commitment to give her life to Him so He could heal her.

I simply have to rest in the knowledge that I did everything I could with the opportunity God gave me that day. I was obedient to the nudging of the Holy Spirit.

That is all the Lord requires of any of us.

Luke

I finished the assembly and waited there in the middle of the gym floor as some four hundred students gathered around in typical fashion. Typical because kids flock to me after an assembly, wanting to talk, hug, cry — anything to get some personal attention. I was enjoying this one-on-one time when the principal walked up with a young man in tow.

"This is Luke, Mr. Roever."

That introduction would profoundly affect my life.

In hushed tones the principal continued, "Luke was found under his house where his father kept him chained. He doesn't speak much, Mr. Roever, but I thought you might want to say something to him."

Luke wore old shoes with no strings, no socks, and blue jeans with holes that were earned the old-fashion way. A faded army jacket partially covered a dingy gray T-shirt. He had a ball cap pulled down low to avoid eye contact and, I presume, to cover his bald head, shaved because of lice.

I'm a hugger. I believe in personal human contact. It stems from my childhood where I found my greatest security in my parents' arms.

I bent down to hug Luke.

I'd scarcely touched him when he jumped back and stiffened. I was shocked. What did I do?

"You can't hug Luke, Mr. Roever," the principal said, then proceeded to tell me why.

No one could hug Luke because of his father. The only time the man unchained him was when he wanted to use Luke for his own deviant purposes. The degenerate savage had sodomized Luke for two years. He'd beaten him into such fear that the boy had lost all sense of reality.

A short time before our visit to the school, Luke had been released from the state hospital, hopefully to be mainstreamed back into society, but it wasn't working. He was ridiculed by peers and laughed at by classmates.

This was the first time I could ever remember being told I couldn't hug a child. I didn't like it. I didn't like the fact that a man could do to a child what the beast had done to Luke.

I had a job to do. I was not going to be denied communication with this boy. I put my hand under his chin, raised Luke's face and looked intently into his troubled eyes. Were they his father's eyes? I hoped not.

"Luke," I said, "I love you."

Did his ears hear me? Or were those the ears of his father — deaf to reality, deaf to love. Was Luke beyond reaching? Was there an ember of hope left in this child?

I said it again, "Luke, I love you."

No response.

I went on, "I'm not going to hurt you. I'm going to hug you.

"Luke, I'm going to put my arms around you. It *will not* hurt, and it's not dirty. Not all men are like your daddy.

"I want you to know I accept you with my embrace, and I welcome you into my world. So, get ready, Luke."

Very carefully I slowly slipped my arms around the residue of an abused, traumatized shell of a human being. His eyes darted wildly around in search of an escape route if escape became necessary, but he didn't jerk away.

Have you ever hugged a telephone pole? My arms were wrapped around rigid sinews and muscle stretched over bone.

I told Luke five more times I loved him. Then I prayed for him.

No response. Aching inside and feeling I'd failed, I turned to walk away when I heard a mumble.

I looked back over my shoulder to see a tear-soaked face on a broken little guy saying two words. "Thank you."

Have you ever seen four hundred kids cry?

Have you ever seen a principal leap for joy even though it wasn't the last day of school?

Have you ever felt like you could laugh till the whole world laughs with you?

I have.

Oh, God, Forgive Me!

Since meeting Luke, I've shared his story in hundreds of public school assemblies. I use the story as a springboard for addressing abuse.

The home I grew up in was filled with Godly love. But I hear statistics tossed around today that tell me what I understood and accepted as normal family life is not even remotely familiar to huge numbers of kids in our society.

These statistics say close to 40 percent of females and 25 percent of males are raped before they reach adulthood. But almost more staggering than the statistics is the fact that most of these atrocities are committed by family members or friends.

Add to those statistics a myriad of teens who are mentally or emotionally abused, and you begin to get a tiny picture of the problems that show up at school every day.

In talking to students about Luke, I openly urge those listening to me to report any kind of abuse to someone in authority.

Then I talk to them about forgiving and explain to them the healing that forgiving brings to one's spirit. I talk about genuine love — a subject totally foreign to many of these kids.

There is something else, though. Luke's story has created a unique opening for bringing up a subject which is considered taboo: praying in public schools.

When sharing Luke's story with high school students, there is rarely a dry eye in the room. The kids are there with me as I try to talk to Luke; they reach out with me when I raise Luke's chin to get him to look me in the eye; they recoil with Luke as he jumps when I try to hug him; they hug Luke with me when he finally lets me touch him; and it's the most natural thing in the world for them to agree with me as I start to pray for Luke.

At that moment in the story, in every assembly, an awesome hush settles over the kids. I pause.

Then I do it.

I fall to my knees... grab my heart... raise my hand toward the sky and cry, "Oh, God, forgive me! I did the unspeakable. I prayed in a public school! Oh, no! Please, God, forgive me!"

Well, when I do that, the place goes wild. Students scream. They stomp. They cheer. They pound on each other. Pure chaos erupts because they see the absurdity of the hype surrounding the issue of prayer in schools.

There are some valuable lessons that I've learned from the story of Luke.

First, principals and teachers are asked to deal with kids who are in desperate situations. But their hands are tied because of restrictions placed upon them as employees of the state. Any principal genuinely concerned for one of his students wouldn't reprimand me for praying for Luke because of Luke's response.

Second, I've learned to be on my toes. In every school the Lord will show me at least one tiny crack in the so-called *wall of separation* erected to keep God out.

And one tiny crack is all I need. I'll keep driving a wedge into that wall until it crumbles and the kids of this nation have the liberty to hear the Truth that will set them free!

I Don't Wike Oo!

There are hundreds of kids with hurts that I have dealt with, but I want to tell you about a girl from a special segment of society with a special set of circumstances — an overlooked group of kids with problems all their own. They are the Down's-Syndrome kids.

Nearly every community where I go has these wonderful, innocent kids in its school system. Helena, Montana, nestled among snow-covered mountains in one of the most breathtakingly beautiful areas of America, is no exception. It was there I met Bethany.

Bethany possessed characteristics typical of victims of Down's Syndrome. Most of them are so vulnerable it's frightening. They haven't learned, or simply do not possess the skills, to couch their thoughts and feelings in deceptive tones or words. I have never known one of them to lie to me. They trust everyone and believe everything they're told.

Even in the impersonal atmosphere of a large assembly, they take everything personally. If I say to the whole assembly, "I love you," they are apt to respond out loud, "I love you, too!"

After the assembly at Helena Junior High, the principal asked me to stay for lunch. I really didn't want to. I hate school food. When I was in school, I didn't like it either. I used to pray over it, "Dear God, please heal it, or kill it. Amen!"

While I was contemplating how to avoid answering the question, the principal ordered my lunch. I never did know what it was. Mystery meat, I guessed.

As the principal and I sat talking about the needs of the students, a small fist hit my right arm, driving my hand into my instant potatoes. Startled, I looked up over my right shoulder to see who had hit me.

There she stood, maybe five-feet-tall, looking intently into my face, determined to communicate her unhappiness with me.

She hit me again. This time my fork went flying into the principal's plate.

"I don't wike oo!" she said.

"You don't like me?"

"Dat's wight," she answered, "I don't wike oo."

"Well, why don't you like me?" I asked.

She paused, looked confused for a moment, then put her thoughts into words.

"I don't wike oo, cuz oo wuv me and den oo weave me."

In the assembly I'd told the entire group of students that I loved them. To her, she was the only person in the room, and I loved *her*. And now I had the gall to leave her!

"I have to leave you," I told her, "but it doesn't mean I don't love you.

"Do you like me now?" I asked.

"I don't wike oo."

"Well, why don't you like me now?"

"Oo ugly," she blurted out.

"I can't help it. Sometimes things happen in life that we don't like, but we can't change them. Do you understand what I'm saying?"

"I know dat."

"If you understand, then you know I can't make the ugly go away." Her eyes never left my face.

I continued, "So, I'm going to make you a deal. I'm going to tell all my friends about you. I'm going to tell them what a wonderful girl you are.

"Do you love me now?"

She thought about it for a while. "O Tay, I wike oo," she said with a nod and a condescending smile.

It's not often I'm caught off guard by kids — I've seen and experienced too much through the years. But I certainly wasn't ready for Bethany's next move.

She threw her arms around my head, caught me in a hammerlock, jumped up-and-down, and shrieked at the top of her lungs, "I never doina till myself adin! I never doina till myself adin! I never doina till myself adin!"

When she finally turned me loose, I righted my hairpiece, re-stuck my plastic ear, and straightened my tie. Trying to get a handle on what was happening, I asked the principal what she was saying.

Grinning from ear-to-ear, he whooped, "She says she's never going to kill herself again!"

I didn't understand. I looked at the principal, question marks all over my face.

He reached over and pushed up her long sleeves, exposing both her arms. Then I understood.

The jagged scar tissue in diminishing shades of red revealed the time intervals between five attempts at suicide.

"I till myself five times," Bethany said sadly, then brightened. "I never doina till myself adin."

Five times she had slashed her wrists trying to commit suicide.

Tears streamed down the principal's face as I held her in my arms. For the first time, ever, Bethany was committing life, not suicide!

I Fight A War, Too

Walter's story is quite similar to Bethany's. In fact the kids were so much alike they differed only in gender. They were about the same age; their speech defects were identical.

And they both had close encounters with Dave Roever in assemblies — encounters which were catalysts for helping them open their hearts to talk.

Somehow, my disfigurement seems to be a point of contact for these kids. I believe it's the scars on the outside they identify with their scars on the inside.

A favorite activity of mine is snow skiing, and most of my favorite ski slopes are in Colorado. So when Summit High in Frisco invited me to come speak, I accepted readily. I knew I could mix a little pleasure with pleasure — ski and speak in a school.

The assembly was the typical, wonderful experience. The students' attitudes were great, making relating to them easy. Even though it was my second time at the school in three years, a majority of the students had never heard me.

At the end of the presentation I opened the forum for questions. Some students asked the typical kinds of things, then Walter stood to his feet. One glance and I knew this could be difficult.

How would the students respond to a Down's-Syndrome student's asking questions?

Would I be able to understand him, or would I embarrass him in front of the whole school by asking him to repeat himself?

I acknowledged his raised hand.

"I fight a war, too," he said. "Eva day, I fight a war!"

I had no trouble understanding this boy. He had to fight every day for acceptance among his peers who excelled in grades, sports, anything, while Walter had to work long and hard to achieve the bare minimum.

I saw the look on the faces of the other students as he started walking toward the stage. They watched to see how I would treat this kid.

I leaped off the stage onto the theater floor.

It was farther down than I realized, and it's a wonder I hadn't broken both my legs! Walter ran to help. He was concerned about me.

I extended my open arms to give him a hug. He threw his arms around me and lifted me off my feet, spun me around and around shouting, "I'm a hero, too!"

The students were crying and clapping madly as they gave Walter his first standing ovation. Walter was a hero at Summit High that day.

He Would Have Been 17 Today

The line of friends extended past the rear exit door of the auditorium. I was tired and more than ready to go to my hotel room, but unless we are flying out after a service, I never leave while people are waiting to talk with me. Some of the most significant moments take place at that time.

Near the end of the line, a patient man with sad eyes waited his turn. He stepped up to me, and I felt uncomfortable as he struggled to find words to broach an obviously difficult subject.

Finally, he bluntly forged ahead.

"My son, Jeffrey, took his life last month, Mr. Roever." He paused, "He would have been 17 today."

Tears filled his eyes. The stoop of his shoulders, the pain etched in his face spoke of such despair, my heart ached for him. I didn't say anything. I didn't know what to say.

"I'm sorry," wouldn't help.

"I know how you feel," would be a lie.

I stood quietly with my hand on his arm and let him talk.

"Jeffrey was a good boy. He had good grades. He didn't have girl problems either. I don't know what happened."

I could hear his anguished soul crying out like a wandering spirit in the desert. Frustrated. Groping. Searching for reasons. As if somehow, a justifiable reason would right things and bring his boy back.

"Could you meet with me tomorrow?" he asked. "I want to show you something."

The man was late for our appointment. He'd stopped by the sheriff's office to pick up the most important thing in his life at that moment: Jeffrey's notebook containing his scrawled suicide note.

One glance at it and my stomach knotted — the cover was sheathed in dried blood. The authorities had taken the notebook as evidence during the investigation, and this would be the man's first look at it. He was afraid to open the cover — afraid of what he would find inside.

As he sat staring at it, he poured out the details of the sordid incident. The scenario tormented him by day and plagued his fitful sleep by night.

"Jeffrey had a shotgun I gave him for Christmas. He liked to bird hunt. That gun was his pride and joy. He got it on December 25th last year.

"On December 21st of this year, he used it to take his life."

He struggled on, each word wrenched by sheer force of will, from an abyss deep in his wounded soul. "My wife and I went to bed at the normal time. I was nearly asleep when I heard Jeffrey slam the door to his bedroom.

"Jeffrey never slammed doors.

"I should have known something was wrong, but I didn't give it another thought. The other sounds I heard didn't register at the moment, but they were the unmistakable sounds of Jeffrey opening the breach of his shotgun and sliding a shell into the chamber.

"The sound of the breach closing sent my mind into a slow-motion panic. I felt the blood rush to my feet, leaving my brain as empty as my spirit. Before the realization of what was happening fully set in, the next sound occurred. A sound that haunts me, especially at night. I wake up in a cold sweat with the same sickening feeling of dread sweeping over me.

He went on, "My four-year-old got to the room first — he is still in counseling — I arrived seconds later.

"Jeffrey's heart was blown out and blood was everywhere. I grabbed him as he was falling over, dying.

"He looked at me with hopeless eyes and said, 'I'm so sorry. I'm so sorry.'"

"I remember clinging to him and crying, 'Jeffrey, I love you! I love you!'

"My God, Dave, it was the first time in his life I ever told him I loved him!"

With the weight of those words almost suffocating him, minutes crawled by before he spoke again.

"Then he slumped in my arms and died. His blood was all over my hands. I looked at them and cried, 'Oh, Jesus, his blood is on my hands!'"

As I sat speechless, listening to the man telling his story, I wondered about my own son and daughter. Had I told them today that I loved them? Did I hold them as long as I could have? Did they try to tell me something I was too busy to hear?

The man opened his son's notebook. Page after page was filled with the art work of young Jeffrey. Most of the drawings were his renditions of rock-music groups' logos such as *Black Sabbath, Guns and Roses, Ozzy, AC / DC*, and others of the same mind (if you can say they have one).

Then the man spoke of himself.

He desperately wanted to compete with his neighbors. New furniture. New cars. You know, all those important things you want in life. None of which matter while holding a dying son.

"I didn't have time to get involved in the things Jeffrey wanted to do," he said. "I was too busy making money. But *I would give it all* if I could just hold him in my arms for even one minute."

Almost a year later, our ministry team was back in that same city holding a crusade at the civic center. After the rally the first night, I was pleased to see Jeffrey's dad.

We visited for few minutes then he said, "Dave, would you go to the school Jeffrey attended and speak to the rest of the students? Four other kids from his class killed themselves. There have been about seventeen teenagers in this city who have committed suicide just this year."

"What? You mean that many students from one class are dead? That many kids from one city?"

It was like an evil spirit had come upon the community. Kids were killing themselves right and left. I couldn't believe it.

"Yes, I'll speak in the school," I told him.

To my surprise, with only one day's notice the school got things in order and had me address the entire student body.

I walked out onto the gym floor and took a quick survey of the students. Some were dressed in black from head-to-foot; some wore chains; some had spiked hair of every color. Some had it all, their outer attire screaming loudly of their inner need for love and attention.

After the assembly, the principal invited the students to the civic center where I would be speaking in an evening rally.

That night the Mayor came, and so did the students and their parents. Over 5000 people jammed into the civic center.

When every seat and the stage behind me filled up, the overflow crowds went into a room to watch on closed-circuit TV. When that filled, another room was opened so people could listen over the P.A. system. Finally the fire marshall locked the doors, and my staff watched as dozens more people came but were turned away.

It just so happened we were in the city the night before Alice Cooper and his band were to present a rock concert with a guillotine on the very stage where I was preaching. I knew the next night the civic center would become a devilish house of the macabre. Young kids' souls would be opened to evils beyond a normal human being's comprehension.

I addressed the crowd, "Folks, tonight you're sitting here in these seats hearing the good news that Jesus Christ sets people free from the powers of sin. Tomorrow night these same seats will be filled with kids from this city who will hear and see the unspeakable depravation sin causes, only it'll be touted as something to be emulated.

"While this building is the *House of God* tonight, it will be the *House of Hell* tomorrow night. What are we going to do about it?"

Pray!

Five thousand people placed their hands on the seats in front of them and asked God to fill the seats with angels. We prayed for God to stop these types of groups from affecting the youth, and we prayed for deliverance for the ones already affected.

Then I preached a message of hope. Hundreds came forward and made commitments to Christ. The power of God won a great victory that night. A father saw something good come out of his family's tragedy: two hundred kids accepted Christ as their Savior.

The next night Alice Cooper showed up ready to take the town by storm. The newspaper carried the account.

Only 200 people came to the concert. Four thousand, eight hundred angels occupied the rest of the seats, so gullible, pliable, impressionable young kids couldn't sit in them!

The Vampire

As I walked into the gymnasium to address one of the largest schools in Minnesota, the atmosphere was stifling, but not with heat or humidity.

On the surface, everything was very much the norm for a high school assembly. The kids sat eagerly waiting to hear what I had to say; no one was moving around or causing any kind of disturbance. But my skin was crawling, and my spirit was churning. I *knew*, without a shred of tangible evidence, that there was a major spiritual war going on in the gym.

Because I was using a wireless microphone, I had full range of the gym floor, so I set out to find the source of the problem.

I paced back and forth as I spoke, my eyes intently studying the faces of the 2000-plus students sitting before me, trying somehow to get a handle on where the problem was. Suddenly, my eye caught an ever-so-slight disruption at the far end of the gymnasium.

As I moved in that direction, it was almost as if I were a kid again playing the "Now you're hot; now you're cold" game. And I knew I was "getting hotter."

My eyes searched each face, row by row. First row: cold. Second row: warmer. Third row: hotter. Then I spotted him.

Our eyes met.

From the top of his hair that was dyed jet black, to his jewelry, to his solid black clothing with its painted-on symbols — he was a Satanist. He looked like a Hollywood imitation of a vampire.

I continued speaking.

The disruptions resumed as the Satanist persisted in his attempts to divert the attention of those around him.

His girl friend, who looked like she had just crawled out of a coffin, was trying to listen, but he was making it impossible for her. He couldn't afford to let her hear what I had to say; she was his compatriot in the occult.

Now, please understand, no one has to listen to me, but in schools I permit no one to interrupt an assembly.

I warned the kid.

He scoffed in contempt.

I jerked off my glasses.

Two thousand kids snapped to rigid attention, muscles taut.

I looked the kid straight in the eye. I looked through him. Let me tell you, there was no love lost between us.

"Kid, look at this face!" I ordered.

"My freedom of speech was earned by the scars on my body, and no one — not you, not anybody else — is going to deny me that freedom. I bought it with my own blood.

"So when I talk, ***you*** shut up! Don't you even breathe unless I tell you to!"

He gasped for breath as though he'd been hit in the stomach. His face turned red, and I realized he wasn't breathing.

"Breathe!" I commanded.

The kids went wild. They stood and clapped and cheered. Someone had finally had the guts to stand up to a Satanist who was trying to destroy their school.

I learned later that dozens of kids had asked the principal to confront the guy, but he wouldn't. What a crime: one kid had been allowed to intimidate a whole school!

The assembly finished on a high note, and I'd turned to walk away when the Satanist flew out of the stands in a rage. He was coming after me.

I didn't see him move (the kids told me), but before he got halfway to me, the football team leaped up and intercepted him.

When I did turn around, all I saw was jet black hair streaking out the gym door.

I don't know what the football team said to him; it doesn't matter. What does matter is that Satan and all his demon forces are no match for the power of God that indwells any one of Jesus' followers.

I Could Have Danced All Night

As I neared the stage to address a southern California public high school audience, I saw a young lady a few rows ahead of me sitting in a wheelchair. When I see students with physical disabilities, I always take a little extra time to talk with them and encourage them.

I approached the girl's chair from behind, and when I turned to greet her, my chin dropped to my kneecaps. I stared in speechless awe.

I'm sure I looked like a fool, but I was stunned by the exquisite beauty of the person who smiled back at me. I tried to speak, but only unintelligible garble escaped my lips.

I was overcome, not by the fact she had lost both her legs as a result of *spina bifida*, but rather by her extraordinary beauty.

Her makeup was flawless, her hair coiffed to perfection, her manicure impeccable, and she sported a smile that would melt the northern ice caps. But hers wasn't just external beauty. The girl radiated with the charm of a gentle and peaceful spirit.

I extended my hand and made another attempt to speak — still, all I could manage was a jumble of gibberish. Like a little boy infatuated with his first-grade teacher, I was falling all over myself.

Her compassion for me seemed to reflect experience. She, no doubt, had dealt with countless others who found themselves in my predicament.

She told me her name. I mumbled something dumb and turned to walk away, still muttering to myself. As I did, I ran into a solid wall of flesh.

He was probably 6'6" with shoulders about three feet wide. Muscles bulged from his folded arms, and the look on his face seemed to suggest I was on his turf.

I smiled lamely, eased around him, and started for the stage again.

Before I stepped up on the platform, a teacher who had been talking with some students, and evidently hadn't seen the encounter, stopped me. "Did you meet the girl in the wheel chair?" she asked.

"Yes," I replied, "She is one of the most beautiful girls I have ever seen."

"And did you meet the young man standing there beside her?"

"You mean the walking wall? Is he a competition weight-lifter or something?"

"No."

Seeing the puzzled look on my face, she told me the story.

"Two years ago he was a skinny nerd who pestered everyone on campus. Then one day he tried to talk to the girl in the wheelchair. When he did, he walked away muttering to himself, totally infatuated.

"From that day on, he started arriving at school just as the janitors were opening the buildings. He'd go straight to the gym and work out in the weight room until the first bell. For two years he's kept at it, all in preparation for last week."

"Oh? Was there a body-builders' contest? Mr. America? Mr. Universe?" I thought I was beginning to understand.

"No. It was the prom."

Totally perplexed, I questioned, "The prom?"

"Yes," the teacher replied, "He worked out for two years, so he could dance with her at the prom. And last week, for two solid hours, he carried her as they danced. Not once did he put her down.

"She has now accepted his proposal of marriage, and we are elated!"

I made my way up on the stage with the thought pounding in my head and in my spirit: Here is a guy who has already chosen to follow the Biblical command which says a husband is "to love his wife as Christ loved the church and lay down his own life for her."

Yes, thank God, there are still millions of decent, loving, caring young people in America who understand true value and worth.

I salute two champions among them!

I Quit!

In the early days of my work in schools, I never knew how to say no. Anytime a school called I would go, regardless of my physical condition. It just wasn't in me to say *no* to an open school. During a single week of one of those early tours I spoke thirty-three times.

We were in the Grand Rapids, Michigan, area and I did a combination of school assemblies and church services. My voice was almost gone. Push as I might, all I could muster was a gravelly, rasping, almost-inaudible level of sound. There were times when I thought I would cough up my vocal cords my throat was so raw.

Sunday night finally came, and we closed out the week of meetings. But I had to move on to Colorado Springs where I had a school assembly scheduled for eight o'clock the next morning.

To arrive there in time, I booked a flight with a 4:00 a.m. departure, then fell into bed.

The alarm sounded with an irritating squeal, setting the tone for my day. I didn't want to move. Common sense said, "Turn off the alarm; go back to sleep."

On top of being totally exhausted, I knew I wouldn't see my family for a week or more. They would be leaving in our bus, traveling in a caravan with our television and lighting trucks.

I dragged myself out of bed, dressed, kissed Brenda and the kids good-bye as they slept, and headed for the airport.

A winter storm was moving through the northern states, causing flight delays and cancellations at O'Hare field in Chicago where I would be changing planes. I was ready to phone Ray Smith who was to pick me up in Colorado and tell him I'd be late or would possibly miss my appointments altogether. I never made the call.

The passengers for the connecting flight, which I thought I would miss because of the weather, were reassigned to the aircraft I was already on!

When I reached Denver, Ray grabbed my baggage, and we hit Interstate-25 in a dead heat to beat the clock. I did three schools and an evening rally, then we loaded up and drove back to Denver to spend the night at Ray's home.

At six the next morning that dreadful sound shattered my sleep again. For the first time since I could remember, I had to use the alarm on a clock radio. The radio itself would no longer awaken me.

My sleep seemed too deep, too heavy. I felt depressed most of the time and slow to respond to humor... totally rundown like a wind-up toy at the end of its mainspring.

Hauling myself into the bathroom, I showered in hopes of sparking some life into my tired body. Then I dressed and stumbled out the door, barely missing Ray.

He yelled over his shoulder as he charged by me, "Gotta hurry. Morning traffic in Denver is a nightmare."

I wished I'd slept long enough to have a nightmare.

The sight of students racing into the parking lot to get the best parking spaces was a familiar sight to me, so I should have noticed my overreaction. "Just like sex, they can't wait to get it," I griped.

Ray and I entered the school, and immediately were caught up and carried along by the flood of humanity surging down the halls. We checked in at the office and chatted briefly with the principal before he escorted us to the gym.

The student population of several thousand had to be divided because the gym wouldn't hold the whole crowd. I was scheduled to do two one-hour assemblies with a fifteen-minute break between them.

The first assembly was a winner. As is the case on every occasion where I find myself at the end of my energy, either physically or emotionally, God gave what I needed to get me through the presentation.

After the first students were dismissed, I stood quietly drinking a cold glass of water, resting before the next group of students would arrive. I glanced up and noticed the principal and Ray talking secretively. Then the principal walked over to me.

"Mr. Roever, the next assembly will be cancelled."

I was stunned. My mind raced. A jumble of statements I'd made in the first assembly echoed in my head. "What did I say? What did I do that displeased him?"

I couldn't believe it. I'd never had an assembly cancelled. When I finally found my voice, I sputtered, "What's wrong?"

I cherish my reputation as a school-assembly speaker and guard it carefully. This could not be happening. I pressured him, dogged his steps, insisted he answer, not realizing I was fast losing control.

When he finally turned in response to my demands, I noticed tears in his eyes. That totally confused me. Ray Smith had reached me by now and stepped between the principal and me.

"What's going on here, Ray?" I demanded.

He pulled me aside and put my back against the boy's locker room door. Ray was weeping openly.

"What?" I wondered, "What could I possibly have done?"

Ray looked me in the eye and said softly, "There's been a death in your family."

The words crashed into my mind like exploding fireworks.

He'd scarcely finished his statement when it hit me. My wife and kids were on the road! All I could imagine was that big bus in a head-on collision with some bigger truck. Who was it? Matt? Kim? Brenda? Who could it be?

My reactions were fine-tuned in training for Vietnam. I grabbed my friend by the throat and reversed our positions. I now had him pinned against the wall, screaming at him, "Don't tell me it's Brenda or my kids!"

Ray clawed at my wrists trying to pull my hands off his throat. "It's your mother! Your mother!" he wheezed.

"Oh, thank God! It's my mother!"

"What am I saying?" Thoughts catapulted over each other, crashing, tearing at my senses.

"It's my mother! The one who brought me into this world. The one whose breast nursed me and upon whose lap I sat in perfect security as a child. It's my mother! My mother!"

I cried at the unspeakable loss. I wanted to be held by someone.

I felt like a little boy desperately looking for Mommy in the supermarket — feeling abandoned and alone. I needed Brenda. My dad. Anyone. I needed someone to hold me. Where was everybody?

My mind struggled, straining for some sort of control. "Pull yourself together, Stupid. You have to finish what you've started. Talk to the principal. You can still do the next assembly. No problem. Poor Dad. I know he's dying inside."

"I'm sorry, Ray," I muttered. "I hope I didn't hurt you."

I heard something being announced on the intercom.

"He's cancelling the assembly, Ray," I moaned. "I could have done it."

I was losing it and couldn't see it. Ray just patted my arm and wept.

I went to the principal's office to find out what to do next.

In the halls a near riot was going on. Students from the first assembly were ecstatic about the program and had poured out into the halls, re-telling my jokes and butchering my punch lines. When the announcement came over the P.A. system that the second assembly was cancelled, pandemonium broke out and students rushed the office demanding they have their assembly. Chaos reigned.

Security was called, and order restored. It was only then the principal announced the reason for the cancellation.

Some of the students turned and held my hands and wept for and with me. Then the principal took me into his office and closed the door.

He extended his arms and embraced me. He held me and wept with me. Not a word was spoken between us — his compassion reached out and touched my grief.

When the initial wave of grief subsided, he called my office and arranged my flight home. As I was leaving, he said, "Don't forget. You have one more assembly to do for me."

I promised him I'd keep his school at the top of my list, then I left for Fort Worth to bury a saint.

The sight of my Dad brought tears again, just when I thought there were no more tears to shed. I shook all over. I believe I was on the brink of a total breakdown.

"How are you holding up, son?" he asked.

"Well, when God took Mom, He almost got two-for-the-price-of-one," I answered.

"Dad, I'm not going to do schools anymore. There's no pay for it, and who gives a rip anyway? I'm tired, and I just want to rest. No more schools."

The funeral was hard. I have never before, nor since, felt such loss in my life. Mom is the only member of our immediate family we've lost. The ache I felt still lingers. When I get really low — tired beyond my ability to encourage myself — I remember.

I cancelled all my engagements for a month. The time off seemed to help. My thoughts were more sane. My sentences didn't ramble disjointedly. And I actually began to look forward to touring again.

But this time, it would be different. I'd do it without all the high-pressure school assemblies where kids come crying, telling you all those stories of abuse.

No more holding hurting kids full of anger from family fights with drunk parents. No more free speeches. Just one promise to keep. That's all. One final school assembly then free at last!

The plane shook and jolted as the tires hit the runway. The drag of wind against the flaps slowed us to a crawl as we edged into the Denver airport terminal.

Thoughts of a month earlier elbowed their way to the front of my mind. This was the last stop before everything would grind to a slow and painful stop. But, stop it would.

Now, just one more school.

Ray met me at the end of the concourse with a broad smile and a greeting of, "Welcome back, Dave, I have seven more schools scheduled for you! Boy, this is going to be a great tour!"

I could have shot him! "What do you mean, seven more schools?"

"Here, let me carry your bags," he said, either not hearing one word I'd said, or by choice, completely ignoring me.

We loaded the bags into the van and turned out of the airport parking lot onto a main street, then onto the Interstate.

"Ray," I began, "I don't think you heard me back at the airport. I want you to know I have decided to stop doing school assemblies. I can't continue the pace. And in all honesty, I don't think anyone cares."

He looked at me like he thought I was kidding.

"No, Ray! Don't look at me like that. I'm not kidding. **I quit**!"

Tears came to his eyes, and he pulled the van off the Interstate onto the shoulder. He put his hands on the top of the steering wheel, dropped his head onto his hands and cried uncontrollably.

"Stop it, Ray. It's not going to work. I quit and that tear act isn't going to change a thing."

"Just when I need you the most," he sobbed. "When I thought I had someone I could count on to help the hurting kids of our state, what do you do? You quit!"

"What are you talking about?" I asked. "When did you need me the most?"

Just the weekend before, he and his wife had taken a trip across the mountains for a visit on the western slope.

"When we arrived late Saturday night, we rented a motel room and collapsed in bed. Around two o'clock, a banging on the other side of the wall awakened us with a start.

"We lay there for a few minutes, trying to collect our thoughts, then it dawned on us. It was the headboard of the bed directly opposite our bed in the adjoining room.

"We smiled at each other and assumed it was the honeymoon suite."

What happened next is not easy to write.

Ray went on, "As the banging continued, suddenly a high pitched scream pierced the night. 'Don't do that Daddy, it hurts! Stop it, Daddy!' Another scream jolted us to the reality of what was happening.

"I knocked the phone off the bedside table as I reached for it. Trying to dial 911, I missed the pad but tried again. Succeeding this time, I yelled into the phone for the police to come quickly — a little girl was being raped by her father.

"The police were there in minutes, but too late to help. When confronted with the accusations, the weeping child, intimidated into submission by the father, denied it all.

"The police left, but not before they apologized. 'We're sorry, it's a family problem and our hands are tied.'"

Gripped with an unspeakable rage as the story unfolded, my insides recoiled with each stab of his words. How could I think of quitting! Not at a time like this! What kind of fool would run away from hurting kids who just want to be given real love?

"Shut up, Ray. I can't take anymore.

"We've got to hurry or we'll be late. We have seven schools to do, you know!"

That was a bunch of years and a few million students ago.

I Touched His Sweat

Through the years, ministering in foreign countries has been an occasional part of my portfolio. Those trips have been anything but vacations, however.

In Israel, I was once chased by a tank. They wanted the exposed film I'd used taking pictures of military installations. I escaped, or rather, eluded my pursuers until I tried to leave the country. It seems they'd taken pictures, too... of me.

I don't have a death wish, but when I travel outside the United States, it's usually to war-torn countries.

After recovering from my injury, I went back to Vietnam while the war was still going on. I worked with U.S.-AID, trying to help the people of the country where I almost lost my life.

I was in the Soviet Union during a coup as one more faction of freedom fighters rose up against the Communist regime. And I've listened to bombs explode during the night in El Salvador.

I've also ministered in Ireland, a country notorious for its on-going civil war that's fueled by terrorists' bombings.

People in these countries understand me because they understand the suffering I have known. They believe a man with an experience as well as a scar.

During my childhood, my father not only pastored churches in South Texas, but he also built Bible schools in Central America. Our family traveled, worked, and ministered throughout Mexico and Guatemala. Because of that, my first language was Spanish. I spoke it fluently until the age of six when I learned English, so I could attend public school in Texas. As a result of these experiences, I have a special affinity for the Latin-American culture.

This story comes with love from a tiny country in Central America where civil war has cost the lives of many thousands. A country where the most beautiful people in the world live. They smile, and you can't help but smile with them. A country where school children don't demand explanations from me. The country? El Salvador.

Letters from the Minister of Education and the Office of the President in that country came, asking me to speak in all the public schools in El Salvador. I felt honored by the invitation to tour their country.

The goal of the Salvadoran Minister of Education was for me to speak to some five-hundred-thousand students during a two-week tour. The government would bus the students into stadiums, theaters, open fields, thousands of students at a time. They would set up P.A. systems and do whatever it took for the students to hear me.

I accepted the invitation with joy, although I knew it would be difficult and expensive. But there was no way I was going to miss the opportunity.

Yes, it meant traveling in dangerous, guerilla-infested areas. The Marxist influence from Cuba and elsewhere kept the political waters of El Salvador in constant turmoil.

During our whole tour of El Salvador, the road to Sonsonate proved to be our biggest obstacle. The danger wasn't so much from the threat of rebel ambush as it was from the crazy drivers of huge passenger busses. The busses were crammed so full the excessive weight was more of a hazard than the excessive speed! It was nothing to see people riding on the tops, clinging to the sides, and hanging out the back doors.

We arrived in Sonsonate to discover that every student in the city was coming to the event. They came marching shoulder-to-shoulder, the full width of the street. As far back as the eye could see, the lines surged forward. Over and over again they packed the theater.

We would finish one assembly, dismiss the students, then another group would jam the place, and we would start again. It was so hot in the theater, perspiration soaked my clothes. The TV camera-men laughed as they watched my clothes change colors on screen.

Finally, the day's events ended, and I was surrounded by beautiful, smiling students. While visiting with them one-on-one, something happened. I didn't understand exactly what until later.

My brother Al, who understands and speaks Spanish much more fluently than I, told me about one girl who came to him.

Notebook paper in hand, she timidly asked, "Do you think Mr. Roever will allow an interview with me for my school newspaper? Do you think he will mind?"

"He will be happy to," Al assured her.

When I saw her, I realized she was the same girl I'd noticed standing about two or three rows back in the crowd of kids wanting to talk to me. She watched me with those beautiful eyes as she patiently waited for her turn.

I felt myself being distracted by her gaze. No matter how I tried, I found it impossible to keep my attention focused on the students who were ahead of her.

She moved up one row, then another, until she was directly in front of me.

Her eyes never left mine. I couldn't believe the warmth I felt or the adoration that flowed from the girl. Then slowly she lifted her hands to my disfigured face and began wiping the sweat from my brow.

Her hand dripped with my perspiration. Tears shimmered on the lower lids of her eyes. A smile spread across her face, and she spun around and ran through the crowd.

Beaming from ear-to-ear, she ran to my brother, "I touched his sweat, and his love entered my heart!"

Spanish is a romance language, you know.

A Precious Loss

As I left the hotel Sunday morning, May 15, 1988, to go to the church where I was to speak, the driver waited for me to pick up a newspaper. At a glance, the headlines told me nothing earth-shattering was taking place. I had forgotten Sunday papers are printed on Saturday, and the best you get is day-old news.

When I got into the car, however, the radio was on. As I was skimming through the paper half-listening to the radio news, I thought I overheard the newscaster mention the name of a familiar town. I snapped to attention. The story was something about a fiery, school-bus crash.

The driver hadn't heard the news report clearly, either, so he changed radio stations hoping to catch the news somewhere else.

It was the top story nation-wide. A story which would change the nation.

It's also a story which should never have to be told. The nation is still trying to bury it with the people who paid the price for the stupidity of one man.

On May 14, 1988, a day that will forever live in infamy, Larry Mahoney started his engine. His day in-and-about Carrollton, Kentucky, revolved around having a few beers here with friends, a few beers there with friends, and, of course, about nine o'clock that night, a six-pack for the road.

The sleepy little community of Carrollton is on Interstate 70 not far from *King's Island,* an amusement park that is usually packed with families out for a day of fun. Among the crowd on May 14th was a bus load of kids, their friends, and sponsors from First Assembly of God Church in Radcliff, Kentucky — 67 of them in all.

The long drive home on the bus that night would be a journey without end. For the families of those passengers, it would be the beginning of a nightmare without end.

Stone-drunk, over twice the legal drinking limit, in fact, Larry Mahoney pulled onto Interstate-70 just outside of Carrollton. There was one major problem, though. In his drunken stupor, Mahoney headed down the wrong side of the Interstate, blind to the error of his way.

What happened next needs no speculation. With no premonition as to what was coming over the hill, John Pearman steered the Radcliff bus on toward home, well within the speed limit.

It took only a few minutes to do what an eternity can never undo. On impact the bus burst into flames and 27 people on board died.

That number included First Assembly's associate pastor, John Pearman, the driver of the bus; and Joy, Kristen, and Robin Williams, the entire family of Sergeant Lee Williams. Dead. All of them.

John Pearman, who was shipped to Vietnam toward the end of the war, never had to pick up a gun or pull the pin on a grenade. He died a wasted death standing in the front of a burning bus trying to pull the pin on a fire extinguisher.

John's 13-year-old daughter, Christy, was one of the passengers on the bus. As Christy's own flesh burned, she screamed for her daddy, and in doing so, inhaled flames and chemicals which virtually destroyed her vocal chords and did internal damage.

Christy lived. But the scars of her body are exceeded only by the emotional scars on her soul.

Brothers and sisters burning. Some living, wishing they were dead. Others escaping only to realize a family member was still on the bus. Twenty-seven people...dead. Most of them kids.

A short time before the crash, I had done assemblies for the Radcliff public schools. John Pearman was youth pastor of First Assembly at that time, and together, we had made plans for another tour for the following year.

As often happens in tragedies such as this, the drunk lived. Larry Mahoney was among the forty-one people who survived the crash, but unlike dozens of the survivors, he suffered few injuries. Today, Mahoney is in prison — though not for long.

The courts did what will never be understood by decent human beings. The jurors found Mahoney guilty all right, but they said the tragedy was not really his fault. It was the fault of the bus. It shouldn't have caught on fire.

That naughty old bus (which, by the way, had just gone through a safety check and passed) was to blame. The court determined that the gas tank was in the wrong place to take a head-on collision. Of course, the company had been putting the gas tanks in the same place for years. And until May 14, 1988, a bus had never killed anyone. But all of a sudden, a bus was to blame.

Hogwash! The bus wasn't drunk. Larry Mahoney was drunk.

Those people were not only ripped from their parents hearts, but from the hearts of everyone who loved them and everyone who would have loved them. And all because one man chose to drink then crawl behind a steering wheel.

When I arrived in Radcliff to speak for a combined funeral for eight of the victims, I was moved by the thousands of people who came to mourn the loss... the precious loss.

I stood to speak and really didn't know what to say. I felt I was there for my dear friend, Pastor Tennison, more than anyone else. Bewildered parents sat in disbelief while I choked on my words. I asked where the beer executives were and demanded that the electronic news media show the footage from the funeral the next time they showed a beer commercial about the "good life."

We buried them that day, but the memory lingers on.

In 1990 Lee Williams put a dozen roses on his daughter's grave. He had promised Kristen that on her sixteenth birthday he would give her flowers.

"A dad's gotta keep his promises, you know," he told me.

Six months after the bus crash, I returned and toured the Radcliff schools again. When the call came asking me to come, I accepted. But what would I do? What would I say to the students? How could I help them deal with the empty desks, the empty lockers, and the voids in their hearts?

As I went from school to school, newsmen from the ABC affiliate in Cincinnati followed me for the two days it took. Tears soaked the cameramen 's faces as they video taped the assemblies and then watched the students weep and hold on to me.

I went into every school where students who were killed on the bus had attended. I saw many of the kids I'd visited in the hospitals immediately following the crash. I saw the little freshman with only one foot — her other burned off in the crash.

And Aaron who was still wearing his Job's mask with eye holes and a mouth hole to breathe through.

And Christy Pearman. She wouldn't play sports or play the piano (two of her favorite things in life) for at least a year. She would spend those hours and days in surgery and therapy to regain the use of her hands and arms.

A year later I went to Radcliff as one of the speakers for a memorial service on the first anniversary of the tragedy.

The state transportation supervisor spoke before I did. He took the stand and began by saying something about the state having passed stringent new laws to protect the good people of Kentucky from any more tragedies of this nature.

"Great," I thought. "Now something will be done about the senseless slaughter of the innocent by the Larry Mahoneys who choose to drink and drive — who kill more people in 24 months than were killed in the whole 10 years of war in Vietnam."

The man continued, "We are demanding that defective busses in this state meet stricter......"

I don't know what he said next.

My mind couldn't get beyond those few words. *What on earth is he doing? He can't be serious!*

People around me sat in stunned silence. The implication of his words knocked the wind out of us. There stood a man, representing the government supposedly "of the people, by the people, ***for*** the people." But like a dog who turns on his master and mauls him to death, the man was ripping the hearts from the people by asserting that 27 people died because of a defective bus.

He knew most of those attending that day weren't accepting such an assessment, but he was preparing the way for court hearings that would divert the process of justice from the true issue of drinking and driving.

Then it was my turn. Thank God for my turn. I took the stand, trembling with rage. How dare the man desecrate this sacred moment with the suggestion that this tragedy was the fault of a defective bus!

I began, "The problem with safety on the highways of Kentucky, or the reason 27 of your loved ones are dead is not defective busses! The problem is defective drunks and politicians who still refuse to accept personal responsibility for their criminal acts of negligence."

That was as far as I got. Some of the crowd leaped to their feet crying and applauding in agreement.

General Tate from Fort Knox stood with tears in his eyes. At his side were the pilots who had flown Sgt. Williams to the grave-side services for his family.

Pastor Tennison from First Assembly of God stood, as did many of the family members of the dead. Of course, those who represented the state Transportation Board weren't standing.

It still strikes me as strange how the political ambitions of men can cause them to devise compromise even in a moment as heart-wrenching as that.

The memorial service over, I left Radcliff. It was easy for me, compared to the families of the 27 dead. They cannot escape the haunting pursuit of loneliness.

From time to time, I have the opportunity to see Lee Williams, and our visits will always end up on the subject of his wife Joy and their girls, Kristen and Robin. Although the pain is still there, God always has an answer.

One day as Lee and I talked, we discussed the plights of different families involved in the rebound of grief and loneliness. Lee told how he would leave the house for days because he couldn't take the constant reminders of his wife and kids. How he ached to hold Joy in his arms, but more than anything else, how he longed to hear the word he now missed the most..."Daddy."

Dottie Pearman not only missed the companionship of her husband, John, but she also missed his leadership.

The three Pearman children, Christy, Robbie, and Tiffany, missed their dad terribly. They needed their dad. John Pearman's death left a gaping void in the children's lives as well as in Dottie's. But God always has an answer.

Lee took a long look at me as though he wanted to ask me about something that was difficult for him to discuss.

Finally, he blurted it out. "Dave, what if I asked Dottie to marry me? She needs a husband, and the kids need a dad."

He went on, "I need a wife, and I miss having children around me. What do you think?"

"Lee, I don't think it matters what I think or what anyone else thinks. This is your life and Dottie's life, and no one else matters except the kids."

Today Lee has a wife and three kids (one more than before, and he has the son he always wanted.) Dottie has a husband, and the kids have a dad. God always has an answer!

Lee said the best Christmas present he has ever received, came the first Christmas after he and Dottie married.

The family had finished opening all their gifts when Christy, the oldest of the three children, said she wanted to say something.

"Lee," she began, "Robbie and Tiffany and I talked, and we know we can never take the place of your kids, and you can never take the place of our dad, but our last Christmas gift to you is, we want to call you Dad."

Sergeant Carter

To provide the best possible service to a community, we like to conclude a day of school assemblies with a night rally. We do this for two reasons. We want parents to come, and we want students to hear the rest of my story.

I feel it does a great disservice to the kids to let them think it was because of my "indomitable human spirit" that I survived my injuries and am doing what I'm doing today. They need to know it was Jesus Christ and the power of God that preserved me, but I can't say that in a public school.

During these evening meetings I am certain to include some tried-and-proven methods to help kids and parents establish lines of communication; to help them deal with the problems of drinking and driving and drugs. I also address any other issue current to that particular community and give a strong message of faith in God as the source of healing for the brokenness in families.

I feel so strongly about the evening rallies, that almost without exception, I require it. Otherwise, I will not book the school assemblies.

We ask as many churches as possible to participate in the night rallies, so the students who choose to make a statement of faith during a rally will have a church of their choice represented. Participating pastors are asked to provide a group of qualified counselors and to support financially if possible, but there are no restrictions if they cannot.

Now the story.

For several years I'd received letters of invitation to go to the schools of Youngstown, Ohio. I had already enjoyed one brief tour in the area, but I couldn't speak for all the schools that wanted me. I promised myself I would return.

There was more to it than that, however. In one school where I spoke, a senior girl of a somewhat-rough cut stepped up to me and rather bluntly stated, "I don't understand you.

"Last year a speaker came to our school and charged us $6000.00. I had to sell stupid candy bars to pay his fee, and he came in here and called us little @#$&*, S.O.B.'s, and $#&*@.

"Now you come in here and don't charge us a penny and tell us that you love us, and we can feel you really do, and you make us laugh and cry, and change our whole school."

By this time her eyes were brimming with tears. She took a quick breath and continued, "I want you to promise me you'll come back and tell my sister, who's two years behind me, the same things you told us today."

Her tears held me hostage. I promised to return.

To my delight, two years later a letter came from a group of pastors in the city, asking me to tour the area schools. I leaped at the opportunity.

As we were making plans to go, though, a nationally-known evangelist made headline news on charges of immorality. The chairman of the Youngstown crusade called and cancelled the event.

When I asked why, he said, "The committee met, and we decided the local churches will handle our local community. We don't need any *evangelist* coming to our town."

"Will you go to the schools?" I asked.

"We will handle our community," was the curt reply.

So be it. It doesn't matter who falls, or what the reason is for the fall. Evangelism did not start with a man, and it won't stop because of the actions of a man. God gave evangelists as a gift to the church.

This evangelist made a promise to a little girl in a school, and I refused to break it just because some narrow-minded preachers couldn't see putting their names on the line.

I called my scheduling department. "Book the first church in the Youngstown area that calls for a rally and schools. I don't care who it is!"

The church that called was Pleasant Valley Church, but we never called it by its actual name. Instead, we called it the *Church-on-the-Farm*. It was way out in the country, miles from town and the schools I would be in — too far away to be a good logical choice for a night rally. The other drawback was, it would only seat about eight-hundred people, packed tightly. We needed a place that had room for at least two thousand.

"Book it anyway," I told my staff. "We're going to Youngstown."

I hit the schools with a fervor, doing every school we could cram into a two-day period. After each assembly, we invited the kids to the Church-on-the-Farm, and they remembered.

The first night the place was overrun with kids. Hundreds were turned away.

It annoyed me because church people were taking up so many seats. I insisted: "Tomorrow night, I want all you church people to stay home and pray for the evening rally. I want you to pray that kids will be set free from habits and bondage to sin." I really tried to impress on them the importance of having room for the kids.

The next day we were back in the schools.

Girard High is in the inner city, and to all appearances, pretty much a *Welcome Back, Cotter* school. I stepped inside the building just as students were leaving one class to report to the next for roll check before coming to the assembly. It was a madhouse.

The principal, a short, stocky man with a flat-top haircut, met me at the door.

"Wow!" I thought, "It's Sergeant Carter."

Sergeant indeed! He never missed a step. "Come with me to my office." He led the way.

Once inside I never sat down. I never received orders to do so.

"How do I pronounce your name?" he barked.

I almost said, "Any way you want to, Sir!" Instead I replied, "Reever."

"Follow me," was his next order. And away he went.

As we entered the auditorium, paper planes strafed the audience from the balcony. Ear-piercing whistles filled the air, and a general uproar of lawless confusion prevailed. But the instant students caught sight of Sergeant Carter, not another sound could be heard.

The last plane made a soft landing, and the principal took his stance at the podium. "I'm here today to introduce to you our speaker, Mister Roever."

With that he stepped over to the stage-left exit and stood there, leaving me facing a gaping group of students staring blankly at me like a calf staring at a new gate.

As I told the story of my injury and subsequent recovery, I kept one eye on Sergeant Carter and the other on the students. Both seemed somewhat unpredictable.

When I mentioned my wife and her love — how she stood by me when I was reduced to a shell of a human being; how she kissed my face and welcomed me home while other wives walked out on their husbands — I noticed Sergeant Carter wiping his eyes. He would turn his back and try to hide it, but the tears kept coming.

He's crying. I knew it; he does have a heart!

At the conclusion of the assembly Sergeant Carter raced by me without ever looking up. "Meet me in my office." His tone hadn't softened a bit.

"Yes, Sir," I thought, "I believe I've heard that order before."

He got there first. The door was open and he was already seated. "Close the door and sit down."

I obeyed.

What happened next is forever imprinted in my memory.

His eyes puddles of tears, Sergeant Carter leaned across his desk and stuttered, "Could I c-come t-to the evening meeting at that Church-on-the-Farm?"

Caught completely off guard, I stuttered. "Of-of course. I would be honored."

That night was the night I told all the church people to stay home. As we turned our bus into the parking lot an hour early, I knew we were in trouble. The parking lot was full and so was the church. Chairs were put out in the foyer, down the halls and any where else space enough could be found.

I stood to speak and found myself scolding the church people for not staying home like I'd told them to. The blank looks on the faces of the people told me I was confusing them.

I asked, "How many of you have never been in this church before?" Every hand in the building went up.

Pastor Cornwall groaned. He didn't own that many visitor's cards.

The rally went smoothly. Like waves in a rising tide, everything built toward the conclusion. Each successive wave building on the last. Finally it came time to give the invitation. I asked for those who wanted to accept Jesus Christ as their Lord and Savior to come to the front of the church. The first man to step out was Sergeant Carter. His wife came with him, and so did an entire row of students from Girard High!

Several hundred students came to know Christ during those two days. But not one pastor from any of those other churches who had cancelled the previous tour showed up. Not one time. Not to a school assembly. Not to a night rally.

Guess who did show up? The younger sister of a girl I had made a promise to two years earlier.

Sorry, pastors, you lose.

Angel Wouldn't Fly

People from all over the nation write to me expressing their love and gratitude for the work I do in schools. What many don't realize, though, is all the work I do is only possible because so many wonderful employees work untiring hours every day to make it all happen.

This is especially true of the men in the cockpit of the corporation's Lear jet. They sometimes fly successive trips with no breaks and often pull 70-hour weeks. After flying all night, they sleep a required number of hours, then go again at full speed. Their days are long and necessitate detailed scheduling of flights as well as never-ending maintenance and inspections.

These pilots are called by God to do what they are doing as much as I am called to do what I am doing. If I've ever missed an appointment because they failed to do their jobs, I don't remember when it was. They are so much a part of the overall picture, I can't conceive of doing what we do without them or *Angel* — the name I 've given our aircraft.

The pilots do much more than fly an airplane, though. They read me like a book. When I get tired, chief pilot, Jim Barnard, notices I start talking about my mother. When my exhaustion exceeds my exuberance, co-pilot, Charlie Burns, will carry my luggage to my room and make me laugh about something on the way.

Both men are my elders (though neither likes to admit it), and I find their wisdom and experience is often the edge I need in making tough decisions. I go to them often for counsel.

Sometimes I make them mad. I don't try to, but they work so hard to make everything just right, and I come along and add people to the flight-passenger manifest, or carry too much luggage to pack properly, or don't show at the appointed departure time.

Such was the case while I was touring schools in the great northwest.

Washington state is beautiful, but it's extremely humid, and during winter the biting cold can make life miserable. On one especially cold, drizzly Sunday night, I spoke, as I usually do on Sundays, in a church. It's churches who support the rest of the week of school activities. I always try to keep on the good side of pastors; they are the key to helping me reach kids in public schools.

After the service on this particular night, the pastor asked my road manager, Monne (rhymes with Johnny) Nidiffer, and I to stay and get a quick bite to eat before we flew on to Portland to do schools the next day.

I really wanted to get to the airport because the pilots were expecting us shortly after 9:00 p.m. I knew they would be waiting with the plane refueled and warmed inside for us, but for some reason I agreed to the pastor's request.

Monne and I left the church with the pastor, ate in 30 minutes, and made the 15-minute trip to the airport, arriving about 45 minutes late. When we got there, no one had to tell me I was in trouble with the pilots. Don't misunderstand me; they are never disrespectful, but they were getting close to being so that night.

What difference does 45 minutes make? A big difference. At 9 o'clock the temperature dropped to 31 degrees and the drizzling rain started freezing on the wings of the Lear. No one flies with ice on wing surfaces; it's certain death to try. The aerodynamics of a plane cannot tolerate even frost on the wings.

After the rain stopped at 9:15, the pilots scraped the entire wing surface by hand — the small airport where the plane was parked had no de-icing equipment. Working like crazy, the pilots had the plane ready by 9:30, thinking we would surely arrive by then. But we didn't show.

Between 9:30 and 9:45 the rain started again, much heavier than before. By the time Monne and I got our things loaded for takeoff, thick ice covered the wings. We all got out and started scraping. Of course, none of us had on the proper clothing for working outside in that kind of weather, so we were freezing.

For nearly two hours we worked without stopping, but as quickly as we scraped an area, the freezing rain would coat it again. Our efforts were futile. This was one night *Angel* wouldn't fly.

Around midnight we gave up and went for hot coffee at a nearby restaurant. Sipping the scalding liquid for another two hours eventually helped us thaw out, but the freezing rain never let up. Bone-weary, I called it a night and suggested we get a room.

We saw a motel across the parking lot and walked over to it, but the place was dark and the little window with a hole in it was closed. What now? The four of us just stood there asleep on our feet. Then I noticed a button to ring for help, but I hated to push because I knew the night clerk would be asleep. I pushed it anyway.

We waited. No response.

I said, "Guys, I really don't want to push that button again. I know it'll get somebody out of bed."

The stillness of the wee hours of the morning was abruptly shattered by a woman's voice from the other side of the window. "I'll get up for you anytime, Dave Roever!"

I almost jumped out of my shoes. Monne's and the pilots' heads snapped up.

Who in the world was that? All of us wanted to find out who was behind that wall.

The woman opened the office door and invited us in. When I saw her, I realized she wasn't someone I knew.

"I watch you every Saturday night," she said. "Your TV program blesses my life. My husband liked you, and you were the only preacher on TV he would watch!"

I thanked her and told her I loved her for helping us. We waited for the room keys, but she wasn't finished talking.

"Since my husband died, I've been running the motel by myself, and it's just too much for me to do alone.

"Tonight I got so depressed I went to bed saying, 'God doesn't love me anymore.' I wanted to give up. Cash it all in because I'm so lonely.

"I lay there in my bed and told God I didn't think He loved me anymore. But if He did, would He please send someone special to tell me.

"And at that exact minute, the buzzer rang. I thought that was mighty fast of God to send somebody that quick. But I got up, and before I ever saw your face, I recognized your voice.

"It was the very man my husband loved to watch on TV. It was you, Davey! God does love me! He sent you here to prove it!"

"Good grief," I thought. "My scheduling department planned this tour two years ago. Twelve school principals and eight pastors are involved. Four different hotels are reserved for the seven nights. The pilots refueled at four different airports. They file flight plans for the flight tonight, but I'm a few minutes late to the airport, and we're grounded, or should I say *iced*, with no hope of departure. And all because one little woman at a tiny little motel in Everett, Washington, thinks God doesn't love her anymore!"

So, what does God do? He sends an ice storm that covers three states, shuts down all my plans, puts thousands of people out of work for a day, closes schools for thousands of students, just to let this woman know He loves her.

Yep.

Oh, by-the-way, the next morning we scraped ice from the wings for an hour, then the airport opened and we used hot water to melt the rest of the ice.

We took off for Portland and landed on a solid sheet of ice, 6000-feet-long. We slid to the terminal, deplaned, got into a car and worked our way through the icy streets to the appointed school. We arrived five minutes early only to learn school had been cancelled for the day!

Women!

God loves them so much He will move heaven and earth to confirm His love to them.

Breaking the Chains

As the diesel smoke from their big bus filled the air, I said good-bye to *One Man's Love*, the band that is such an important part of our crusade ministry team. I watched as they pulled out onto the road headed for California via Phoenix; then I breathed a prayer for their safety and turned and walked back into the building.

I recall the first time I used *One Man's Love* to do the music in a crusade. I was astounded by the way people responded to them.

Until that time, I'd never really considered the impact of music on an audience. I basically thought music was just something you did to fill time while people were gathering for a meeting. I knew music would entertain, or, if you were lucky, it might even minister to the folks, but I'd never stopped to weigh its actual influence.

One Man's Love, whose members range in age from 19 to 28, would change the direction of our crusades forever. They are the hottest band I have ever seen for reaching young people who aren't familiar with church or religion. Since *One Man's Love* has been with us, there has been a huge increase in the number of teens coming to our crusades. And the number of them responding to the invitations to accept Christ as Lord and Savior of their lives has doubled.

With the band in place and with my two associate evangelists, Reggie Dabbs and Phil Chapin, going full time, I thought all the members of the best possible ministry team were assembled, but God surprised me.

Six months earlier, the band returned from a youth camp raving about the talents of a guy they'd met named Randy Phillips. They couldn't stop talking about Randy and the excellent job he does as a *Human Video* — the term Randy likes to use when referring to his work in mime.

At the band's insistence, I finally called Randy and asked him to do a tour in California with us which would include public-school assemblies.

Randy said he had a concept he thought would be perfect for schools, but he would need help from the members of the band to make it work.

Six years ago he'd come up with the idea of doing a drama using chains to depict bondages to drugs, alcohol, pornography, and violence. Even though Randy had never done a school assembly or hadn't had an opportunity to use the idea, he said he was ready.

The band members were also excited about being involved in a public school assembly for the first time.

One Man's Love stopped in Phoenix and picked up Randy then continued on to Northern California where they joined me.

With the band, a sound man, two associate speakers, two pilots, me, and now Randy, the entourage was getting so large I began to wonder how I would feed them all.

The time for the first assembly of the tour finally came, and I was introduced to the students.

I gave a condensed version of the story of my injury and miraculous recovery, then ended by saying, "I refuse to follow the trends of so many Vietnam vets and turn to drugs and alcohol to try to drown the past. I refuse to beat my wife. I refuse to spend the rest of my life in a prison, or commit suicide as so many vets have done. My decision was to break the chains of the socially unacceptable behavior of a Vietnam vet and enjoy my life and my family and wear real clothes."

Then I introduced my associate, Phil Chapin, who told of his childhood ordeal. Phil was born to a 16-year-old heroin addict who started giving him marijuana when he was six to control his hyperactivity.

Phil told of the abuse he took at the hands of his father, who in fits of rage, would beat him into unconsciousness. The state of California took Phil and put him in a juvenile detention facility, then finally sent him to Oregon to live with an aunt. While attending a private school there, Phil met Lonnie Chapin who invited him to his house to meet a "real" family. The Chapin family took Phil in, loved him, and eventually adopted him.

Today Phil goes with me into schools and explains to students that if they are abused, they don't have to continue that cycle of abuse and become abusers themselves. He assures students they can break the chains of abuse.

When Phil finished speaking, I introduced my other associate, Reggie Dabbs.

Reggie was born to a teenager who was paid $20 to have sex. He is black and can relate to students who share his scars as well as his color. Just one day away from being aborted, Reggie's life was spared by a high school English teacher who convinced the girl to deliver the baby. When Reggie was born, his birth mother rejected him, but the teacher and her husband adopted Reggie and raised him in a caring, loving home.

Statistics say Reggie should be a loser; that he should have grown up to be violent; that he should be one of those who robs the local 7-Eleven for $22.10, goes to prison, and falls in love with a boy named Butch.

Why didn't he? Because, as Reggie tells a quarter-of-a-million students a year, he broke the chains that hold a man in bondage.

As he was wrapping up his portion of the assembly, Reggie looked up into the bleachers and spotted Randy who had slipped in and was sitting with the students.

Reggie said, "Hey, Kid!"

Randy pointed to himself and mouthed, "Who? Me?"

"Yeah, you. How come I'm down here sweatin' and you're sittin' up there in a leather jacket? Come down here a minute."

Wearing a Michael Jordan ball cap, a Michael Jordan T-shirt, jeans, and Air-Jordan shoes, youthful-looking, 28-year-old Randy fit the role of a typical high school student.

As he bounded up on stage, Reggie said, "I'm tellin' you, kids, you don't have to end up like your parents. Take this kid for instance. Say, maybe, his mom is a prostitute. Well, just because his mom is a prostitute doesn't mean that he has to prostitute himself. He can break the chain; he can be something different."

As Reggie talked, the guys in the band, dressed all in black, with nylon stockings over their heads to distort their features, slipped on stage.

Reggie continued, "Or, just because his dad, maybe, is an alcoholic, doesn't mean he has to be an alcoholic. The only way he can become an alcoholic is if he chooses to be one."

Precisely on cue, to Randy's horror, the band's drummer, Dave Wampler, slapped a huge chain around

Randy's ankles, fastened it tightly, and slipped away.

Reggie moved off into the background as Wampler and the other band members returned with pieces of rubber hose and began a relentless, realistic-looking attack on Randy. Every time they struck Randy with the rubber hoses, the loud popping noise caused the audience to wince.

His attackers forced Randy to snort "cocaine," look at "pornography," have "drugs" shot into his veins, etc. As each act was accomplished, they wrapped another huge chain around Randy's body until he was shackled from head to foot with those enormous chains.

The scene was brutal. In fact, the acting was so believable, a teacher told us later that students sitting next to her asked permission to go help Randy.

Their job finished, the band members danced off the stage in triumph, leaving Randy lying limp on the floor.

In the stillness that followed I could hear students weeping for Randy, but I knew in reality they were weeping for themselves.

As he tried to stand, Randy fell again and again. Somewhere in the background the strains of a song began to swell "....gonna break these chains and get back on my feet again."

But try as he might, Randy couldn't free himself. The agony on his face ripped at the hearts of the spectators.

We let him struggle for what seemed an eternity, then Phil slipped over to him and took off one of his chains. Reggie released another; I undid one; then teachers joined in, and finally the last chain was removed by the principal.

Many students were on their feet crying and clapping and cheering. Others were lying on the gym floor weeping uncontrollably.

School counselors were stunned to see the shell on some of their toughest students finally breaking. Kids who never dared shed the masks that concealed their deepest hurts were now expressing raw emotion.

We were overwhelmed to see public-school students touched so deeply.

After our team visited with the kids one-on-one, we packed the props and headed for the van. When I got there, I noticed Phil wasn't with us and went to find him.

I finally spotted him over to the side talking with a girl who appeared to be crying. Knowing something important was probably happening with her, I didn't bother him and went on and got into the van.

When Phil came, he stepped up into the van, and sat quietly for a moment before he opened his hand. In it was a sturdy chain about 8-feet long.

The girl had given it to him, explaining she'd intended to use it that day to hang herself.

She'd carefully made her plans: after school she would go to the band hall, close the door, secure the chain somehow, and end it all.

I'd never in my life heard of anyone hanging himself with a chain, but it was obvious the girl meant business.

We beat the clock this time, but other kids haven't been so fortunate.

I was two hours late in Odessa. The assembly started at 8:30 a.m. The senior killed himself at 6:30.

When I stopped the car at a Sacramento school where I was scheduled to do an assembly, I wondered what was going on. Students were stumbling over each other as they ran to the back side of the school grounds near the tennis courts.

I was too late again. The boy hanged himself on the top of a chain-link fence.

I walked up to the door of a school in Boise, Idaho, just as paramedics whisked a girl, or her remains, out the door. I never did learn whether she succeeded in her attempt at suicide.

I don't take my work in schools lightly. I don't believe God takes it lightly either. In fact, I believe that six years ago God gave Randy the idea of using chains to depict bondages and addictions, knowing full-well that it would not be used until recently.

Only God could possibly have known that I would ask Randy to do a tour with me which included a school where a little girl planned to hang herself with a chain.

Today there is a chain in my office that won't let me forget the reasons I speak in schools.

Schools are the only places in America where kids have to gather every day, Monday-through-Friday for nine months out of the year. Someone has to be there to help them understand.

They ***can*** break the chains of bondage to futures they really don't want.

Who Is Jack Mott?

Niceville, Florida. Sounds like a *Reader's Digest* town. A place where white picket fences line streets laid out north-to-south and east-to-west with oak trees down both sides. A place where one might expect to see an old man walking his dog while telling his grandson about his first train ride, or telling him some yarn about World War II.

As a sister-town to Fort Walton Beach and co-host to the largest Air Force base in the world, Eglin Air Force Base, Niceville has more than its share of problems.

My office received a call for help from a concerned individual in Niceville who said he'd just lost one of his Sunday school students to suicide. Usually we get those kinds of calls from high school teachers or principals, not Sunday school teachers. I wanted to know more.

Jack Mott's urgent plea for us to come do assemblies in the local schools touched the hearts of my staff. It seemed the man cared more about the loss of the boy and the hurt to the family than he did about how something like this might reflect on him.

He wasn't blaming the school system or the parents, nor was he looking for excuses. He did want to know why a 17-year-old boy who sat across the table from him on Sunday, took his life on Monday. However, the boy left no clues; the only thing anyone knew for sure was the cause of his death.

When Jack Mott called, he didn't seem concerned about the cost of bringing our team of speakers into the schools. And he didn't seem concerned about whether or not the schools would even allow us in. His only concern was to do everything in his power to keep another kid from killing himself.

Around 150,000 people live in the Niceville area, and many of them had contact with the 17-year-old suicide victim every day. Jack Mott could have called for help from anyone of them. Or, any of them could have called for outside help. Why Jack Mott, the Sunday school teacher? And why did he call me?

Who in the world is Jack Mott?

Jack Mott is the son of Jack Mott, Sr., who is a sign builder, as is Jack Mott, Jr. And I suspect Jack III (Jay) will be a sign builder one day, too. Remember, this is Niceville. Things don't move too quickly here, and if something ain't broke, don't fix it.

Jack Mott, Sr. serves on the visitation committee for the First Baptist Church where Jack, Jr. is a deacon and teaches Sunday school, and Jay attends Vacation Bible School. This tradition will no doubt continue, and after Jack, Sr. passes on, Jack, Jr. will fill the visitation committee post, and Jay will teach Sunday school and serve on the deacon board, and his son will attend Vacation Bible School.

If all this sounds boring, just remember, there is one family in Niceville who doesn't think so. They would give the whole world to have that boring tradition to look forward to in generations to come. But their hope died on Monday.

Who is Jack Mott?

He is tradition. Jack Mott is order. He is stability. Jack Mott is the past and the future all wrapped up in the present. He is a man with a heart as big as Niceville. A man with a heart for the kid who looks at his dad and cannot find himself in his father's eyes.

When Jack called my office, we realized this man wanted the impossible. He wanted me to come to speak in the Niceville area schools — schools that knew nothing of his intentions, that knew nothing of my objectives for a high-school assembly, and that certainly knew nothing of my ways of dealing with the delicate subject of suicide.

Jack also wanted to secure the high-school stadium for a night rally and wanted 50 churches from 15-or-so denominational backgrounds to participate in the event. And he wanted it all done ***in 10 days***.

To start with, I have a full-time scheduling office that keeps my calendar set for the next two years, not just the next two weeks. To get a school stadium for a religious event could take an act of Congress, and to get 50 churches to work together on anything could take an act of God!

School calendars are usually set a year in advance and are not usually subject to change. Furthermore, a few years earlier, a Jewish family in the Niceville area had taken great offense over a preacher speaking in an assembly and had sued the school district. The case went all the way to the U.S. Supreme Court, and the school lost.

To say the school was gun-shy about having another preacher enter their doors is an understatement. There was just no way to expect this event to come off.

Everybody knew it wouldn't fly — everybody, that is, except Jack Mott. Well, one other guy sorta believed it could happen.

I told my scheduling department to book the request no matter what it took on our part. And it proved to be a major undertaking. Every shred of reasoning and experience was stacked against the Niceville effort coming off.

First, the geographical location was the opposite direction from where I was needing to go.

Second, our ministry had no previous connection to the people there. We didn't know who to put in charge of coordinating things in Niceville. Who would the local people trust? We needed someone to chair the event who could cross denominational lines without offense; someone who wouldn't accept "No" for an answer from a school principal; someone who would know the right people in the superintendent's office; someone with a history of accountability and tradition, and someone with a heart for the kids.

Jack Mott. Who else?

We landed at a small airport about fifteen miles north of Niceville close to midnight on Sunday night. Totally exhausted from a weekend of special events, I really began to wonder if I were doing the right thing. Were we crazy for coming here on such short notice?

Jack Mott and his long-time friend, Bob Mathers, greeted us as we got off the plane. My first impressions were wonderful. Both men had an exuberance about them that was contagious and reassuring. I lost all apprehension about the upcoming crusade and focused my attention on the reports the men were giving. They told us of incredible victories in the schools and churches.

Jack and Bob were like boys with stories of big game hunts. They said their first requests for assemblies were turned down flat by the schools. Then, out of no where, the assistant superintendent called, saying she had seen the video of my high school presentation and had showed it to the school board. The board voted unanimously to have me come.

Jack and Bob were ecstatic over being able to secure the football stadium and the city-owned platform used for graduation. Not only were they given permission to use the platform, but city workers would be setting it up in the stadium the next day!

The men weren't in suits and ties when they came to pick us up. They wore jeans and boots and were driving a 4-wheel-drive truck which banged along with something broken in the drive line. I laughed out loud! I loved every minute of it. These were real men. And they certainly weren't trying to impress me with appearances and egos. I knew this would be a great crusade and school tour.

I rested well that night and awakened feeling surprisingly refreshed after such a long, tiring weekend.

After breakfast, Jack and Bob picked us up, their spirits soaring high with excitement over what they felt the Lord was going to do during the day we were facing. None of our expectations, however, would come close to what actually happened.

The first school was a smashing success. The students were pumped and ready for me. They responded to everything I said. Despite worries about past court cases, the administrators were cordial and receptive. After the assembly, students picked up fliers advertising the evening rally in the stadium and promised to show up.

From there we went to the First Baptist Church for a luncheon where some 50 pastors were waiting to meet with me. My eyes were seeing it, but my head was having a hard time believing it! How could this be happening?

Who is this Jack Mott?

How did he pull it off?

Pastors and priests hugged each other, prayed for one another, and prayed for all the churches. They listened intently for almost an hour as I spoke of the needs in their schools and gave them the simple solution to a complex problem.

As I spoke, I was interrupted three times by urgent phone calls for different pastors in the room. One call was to inform a pastor that a local pornographer had just put out a death threat on him.

The other calls were about two more attempted suicides which happened as we were gathered there. It all served to underscore the nature of the problems that had brought us together.

The luncheon ended with prayer, and we were off to the next school where the recent suicide and attempted suicides had taken place.

As the principal was trying to get the attention of the students who were packed so tightly in the gym some had to sit on the floor, the microphone cable broke. I thought I was dead in the water. No way were we going to be able to fix the cable without losing the students in the process.

Not ten seconds later a man from the church across the street stepped up and said, "Dave, I thought you might want a longer wire than the cord the school uses, so I brought you this one."

I looked from the 10-foot broken cord to the one he was holding. I not only had a cable that worked, but now I had enough wire to reach across the entire gym floor! God knew I would need it.

In the top of the bleachers at the far end of the gym were the trouble makers who wanted to take over the assembly. I knew this was no coincidence. The boys tried the usual tricks for disrupting a speech and throwing a speaker off his stride. But they had no idea what they were in for when they started this time. They'd never tangled with a Doberman Pincer before! I won the admiration of the entire school by controlling a gang of boys who thought they were men. The assembly was made in heaven.

When I finished, the kids gave a standing ovation while they whistled and screamed their approval. I invited them to pick up fliers about the stadium event that evening, and they took every one we brought.

Now it was time to see what God could do with just 10 days of preparation and prayer. No longer would we wonder if moving on the suicide problem quickly was wisdom. Our hopes to arrest this senseless death pattern were on the line. Would anyone show that night, or would all the efforts of Jack Mott be wasted?

As we approached the stadium that evening, I saw a long line of vehicles whose turn signals flashed the good news that a miracle was taking place. Hundreds of cars were lined up to unload passengers or to find parking spaces. Busses were moving like a caravan into the area designated for them.

Even though the temperature hovered around 40 degrees, making it a miserably cold night for Florida, around 4,500 kids and parents showed up!

I was taken to the back entrance and ushered to the platform the city had erected on the 50-yard line. Then I saw the first problem. And it was one with disastrous proportions. The sound system for the event was grossly inadequate.

We needed sound to cover an entire side of a football stadium. Because there are no walls to contain the sound, the size of a sound system has to be tripled or quadrupled. For me to be heard, we needed at least ten large speakers and five heavy-duty amplifiers. What we had was exactly two speakers, maybe two-feet tall. The one power source served as both amplifier and control board.

I was almost sick to my stomach. So much work, so many prayers — not to mention money. All the scheduling changes and school miracles — all down the drain. How could the crusade continue? Beyond the first row, no one would be able to hear a thing.

There was no time to worry. Thousands of people had gathered to hear from God through the man who would bring them His Word. I would give it all I had. I took the microphone and saw a miracle happen as surely as the one that happened when Jesus feed 5000 people with five loaves of bread and a couple of fish. I was heard across the entire stadium!

I double checked to make sure. I asked if those in the upper corners could hear. They roared back with applause and shouts of praise. I don't know why I was surprised. After all, weren't we working with Jack Mott?

The people were attentive as I preached the message I felt God wanted me to share with them. As I gave the invitation, tears streamed down my face. Kids poured out into the aisles and came to give their lives to Christ. Weeping Vietnam veterans came with their wives and kids. This could only be the work of God.

The area around the platform there on the football field was filled as counselors and respondents sat in the grass, holding hands and praying together. I walked among them and listened to some of the conversations and prayers.

One girl was laughing and crying at the same time. When I stopped to ask what was happening, she told me that late that morning she had attempted suicide but was restrained by friends and family. She was one of the kids we'd gotten a call about during the pastors' luncheon.

The first fruit of all the prayers and all the effort, of all the tears and all the money spent was sitting in the middle of the football field, crying for joy and bubbling with laughter because she now had a reason to live!

I moved over closer to the stage, and there were the parents of the boy who had killed himself.

Those poor people carried a grief I could never fully understand unless, God forbid, I were to walk through a similar ordeal. They looked across the people coming to Christ, 112 decisions in all, three or four of whom had been contemplating suicide. They looked at the girl who just that morning had tried to follow their son in death. They watched as she rejoiced in her new-found a reason to live. Out of their tragedy they were beginning to see a glimmer of triumph.

I moved on. As I stepped up to a Vietnam vet who stood holding his wife in one arm and his daughter in the other, he said, "For the first time since the war, I am really home."

At the back of the crowd standing on the field was a group of boys dressed in black Raiders jackets — the local gang who got too close to the creek bank that night and slid in. Arm-in-arm they stood listening as an old lady told them of the saving power of Jesus Christ.

Eventually the crowd began to dissipate. People were going home, different. They were going home with hope. They were going home with Jesus in their hearts.

Where was Jack Mott?

He was over behind the stage stacking chairs, loading equipment, and rolling up sound wires, never asking for glory or even a thank you.

Who is Jack Mott?

Just a man doing what has to be done.

Questions

At the end of assembly presentations, if the school administrators will allow it, I open the floor for questions. Kids are frank, outspoken, and generally up-front with their questions. This book wouldn't be complete without giving you a sampling of some of those sessions.

Student: How did you get started doing school assemblies?

Dave: A teacher in Indiana walked up to me and asked if I would come to his school and speak to his sociology students. When I asked why he wanted me, he said they were studying Vietnam veterans. I asked him if they dissected in sociology. He laughed and said no, so I went. I never expected the students to do what they did. They laughed and cried and gave me a standing ovation! The principal was auditing the class because he wasn't sure about what might happen with a 100-percent-disabled Vietnam veteran in his school. As a result of that session, the principal invited me to speak for graduation, and from that time on, I have stayed booked in schools for two years in advance.

Student: Sir, what was the first thing to go through your mind when the grenade exploded?

Dave: Shrapnel!

Student: Why do you go to schools when you know there is no money in it for you?

Dave: First of all, I love you. But if I come in here and tell you I love you, then you see me getting paid for it, you would think I was paid to love you. If I were paid to love you, then I'd be a prostitute. And I don't have a short skirt! (They like it when I talk dirty.) Second, if I take federal funds for speaking in schools, Uncle Sam could step in at any time and tell me what to say, when to say it, how to say it, or tell me not to say it at all. If for no one else in the world, I bought my own freedom of speech in Vietnam with every aching scar on my body, and I refuse to sell it for thirty pieces of state silver.

Student: Are you married, and do you have children?

Dave: I was married before I went to war. We had no children prior to the war because we chose not to risk having a family until I knew the demands the military would put on me. In other words, I didn't want to leave my wife to raise children alone if I were to die in Vietnam. However, following the war, my injury required 14 months of hospitalization. The doctors told me on my very last day in the hospital that my injury had probably rendered me sterile, which is a common occurance among burn patients. Well, I'm happy to tell you that my genes may have been damaged, but they weren't dead! I have two kids. They're mine, too. They look just like me...plastic ears and everything!

Student: Do you ever get depressed?

Dave: Yes. When I get depressed, I don't do drugs; I do a school. That always gets me high!

Student: Have you ever done drugs?

Dave: I am 45 years old. I've been to hell and back; I've stared the death angel in the eye till he blinked, and I did it drug-free and alcohol-free. If I can, so can you! I've never smoked a joint in my life. I've never snorted coke. The only coke that's ever been in my nose was when I was drinking it and sneezed. Wow, that was a bad trip!

Student: What do you think about Planned Parenthood's program of using bananas to demonstrate the use of condoms?

Dave: I think it's really great. I think bananas should always use protection! I do feel however, that someone should tell the bananas that good percentage of condoms fail, and a banana with HIV infection that leads to AIDS is a very unhappy banana!

Student: Sir, do you believe in Jesus Christ, and do you feel He is the reason you are alive today? (The kid was not a plant in the audience, really!)

Dave: Because you asked, I have the freedom to express myself on this matter. Let me say this: you have asked a question in search of truth, which is what education is all about. Yes, Jesus Christ is the reason I am alive. My faith in Him has never failed me because He has never failed me.

Dave: (To a principal when during an assembly a girl sang a song about the blood of Jesus never losing its power.) Dr. Brown, did you know she was going to sing that song?

Principal: Of course. I requested it.

Dave: How can you get by with such a thing when people are so rigid about the so-called "separation of church and state"?

Principal: It's easy. I retire in two weeks!

Desensitized

By now you're probably glad this book is coming to an end because you've grown weary of the emotional drain which comes from reading so many heart-wrenching stories. The same thing happened to me when I watched a television special on satanism.

The show produced in me a nausea so strong I wondered if I could take more than a few minutes of its horrible content. But I forced myself to watch.

And then I noticed a strange desensitization taking place in me. The more bizarre the program became, the more my mind rejected it — not the truth of it, but the pain of it. I couldn't believe I was watching such descriptions of mutilations and murder. I just sat there staring, much like the story of the frog in hot water.

When the frog was placed in a tub of cold water, he was content, but when placed in hot water, he jumped out. He was then put into a tub of cold water and the temperature was slowly raised to the boiling point, and the frog died.

I, also, adjusted to the temperature of my environment. My natural reactions were seared by over exposure.

What happened to you as you read this book? Did you become desensitized? Were there tears in your eyes as you read about Luke and Sarah? Were they still there when you read about the girl in Colorado who was raped by her father?

I'm not trying to put you on a guilt trip. But if it all seems too much, and you're ready to close this book and forget what you've read, remember, there is no such reprieve for the victims.

They can't close the book and be finished with the ugliness. Nor can I so easily lay down the memories. They haunt me each night, forcing me to wonder if I've done all I could during that day to stop the pain for at least a few kids.

More than anything else, it's the look in their eyes that gets to me. Just today at Centennial High in Minneapolis, it happened again.

She was, maybe, seventeen-years-old and waited until everyone had finished talking. I was one step from the door, ready to leave, when she moved closer to me and asked, "Mr. Roever, do you have a minute?"

I always have a minute.

What would she reveal? What deep, dark sin against her would she expose?